Hacking Medical IoT: Security Risks in Smart Healthcare Devices

Zephyrion Stravos

Imagine this: You're in a hospital, wires beeping, machines humming, doctors and nurses bustling around. Everything seems... normal. Safe. Professional.

But what if I told you that, somewhere in this sterile, high-tech fortress of healing, a hacker could be playing Flappy Bird on a pacemaker?

Okay, maybe not Flappy Bird. But you get the idea.

Welcome to **Hacking Medical IoT: Security Risks in Smart Healthcare Devices**, a deep dive into the vulnerabilities lurking in smart medical technology—the pacemakers, insulin pumps, infusion machines, and hospital networks that keep millions of people alive every day. You'd think these life-saving devices would have Fort Knox-level security, right? Nope. Turns out, some of them are about as secure as a diary with a broken lock.

But before we start dissecting medical IoT like a hacker performing an unauthorized autopsy, let's talk about why this book exists.

Who Am I and Why Am I Dragging You into This?

I'm Zephyrion Stravos, a guy who has spent way too much time poking, prodding, and occasionally breaking IoT devices. I live at the intersection of curiosity and chaos, which is exactly where you need to be if you want to understand the world of hacking. And let's be clear—this isn't just about breaking things for fun (though, let's be honest, that's a perk). It's about making things better by exposing their flaws before the bad guys do.

This book is part of my IoT Red Teaming: Offensive and Defensive Strategies series, where we go beyond the usual "change your password, update your software" security tips and get our hands dirty with real-world hacking techniques. If this is your first rodeo with me, welcome aboard! If you've already read Mastering Hardware Hacking, Firmware Hacking & Reverse Engineering, or Wireless Hacking Unleashed, then you know the drill: We don't just talk about security. We break things to understand how to secure them.

And today, we're turning our attention to one of the most terrifying hacking targets out there—your health.

Medical IoT: Where Security Takes a Backseat to Convenience

Medical IoT (or MIoT, because every field needs an acronym) is the fusion of healthcare and technology. It's what lets doctors monitor patients remotely, automate treatments, and streamline hospital operations. Sounds great, right? In theory, yes. But in practice? It's a hacker's playground.

Why? Because the healthcare industry has a fatal flaw—it prioritizes patient care over cybersecurity. Which makes sense… until a ransomware attack locks down an entire hospital's system, forcing doctors to fax prescriptions like it's 1995. Or worse, when an attacker exploits an insulin pump's wireless connection to deliver a fatal overdose.

I'm not making this up. These attacks have already happened. And the worst part? It's just the beginning.

Attackers Love Medical IoT, and Here's Why

Let's play a quick game of Why Would a Hacker Care? Here's what medical IoT offers to attackers:

- **Weak Security by Design** – Many medical devices were designed before cybersecurity was even a concern. Updating them? Not always an option.
- **Massive Attack Surface** – Hospitals are like a hacker's buffet: patient records, connected devices, unsecured networks—take your pick.
- **Life-and-Death Stakes** – If a smart fridge gets hacked, your ice cream melts. If a pacemaker gets hacked, someone dies. That's a whole new level of leverage for cybercriminals.
- **High Ransom Potential** – Attackers know hospitals must function. That's why ransomware groups love targeting them—because they'll pay.

And if you think, Well, surely the government has this under control, let me introduce you to the wonderful world of outdated regulations. HIPAA? FDA guidelines? IEC 62304? They exist, sure. But security in MIoT is like a seatbelt in a car made of paper—it's there, but it's not gonna save you in a crash.

What You'll Learn in This Book (Besides How to Terrify Your Doctor)

This book is a no-BS, hands-on guide to hacking and securing medical IoT. Whether you're a pentester, a security researcher, or just someone morbidly curious about how easy it is to mess with a hospital's MRI machine, you're in the right place.

Here's what we'll cover:

- **The Growing Threat Landscape** – Why hospitals are prime hacking targets and how attackers gain access.
- **Medical IoT Architecture** – The nuts and bolts of connected healthcare devices and networks.
- **Hacking Techniques** – Everything from network reconnaissance to wireless attacks on pacemakers (yes, really).
- **Cloud and API Exploits** – Because telemedicine and remote monitoring are the future… and also riddled with vulnerabilities.
- **Ransomware, Malware, and Backdoors** – The nastiest threats lurking in medical IoT.
- **Physical and Side-Channel Attacks** – How bad actors can extract data without ever touching a network.
- **How to Fight Back** – Defensive strategies for securing devices, networks, and patient data.

By the time you finish this book, you'll be able to think like an attacker, exploit vulnerabilities like a pro, and (hopefully) use that knowledge to protect medical IoT rather than, you know… becoming the villain in a cyber-thriller.

A Quick Disclaimer (Because Lawyers Exist)

This book is for educational purposes only. If you're here because you want to hack your neighbor's insulin pump for fun, close this book and rethink your life choices. Ethical hacking is about making technology safer, not using it to cause harm. The techniques we discuss should be used in controlled environments, with proper authorization, and for the greater good.

Now that we've covered the obligatory "don't be a criminal" warning… let's get hacking.

Chapter 1: Introduction to Medical IoT Security

Imagine walking into a hospital where everything is smart—smart beds, smart IV drips, even smart toilets that analyze your... outputs in real time. It sounds like a sci-fi dream until you realize half these devices are running outdated software, have default admin passwords like "1234," and can be hacked faster than you can say "medical malpractice lawsuit." Welcome to the world of Medical IoT (MIoT), where life-saving devices meet security risks that could make even the most seasoned hacker's jaw drop.

Medical IoT security is the study of protecting connected healthcare devices, networks, and data from cyber threats. These include everything from wearable health monitors and insulin pumps to hospital networks and cloud-based patient records. As medical technology advances, so do the risks—making it crucial for security professionals, healthcare providers, and researchers to understand attack vectors, vulnerabilities, and defense mechanisms. This chapter provides an overview of MIoT, its rapid growth, and the challenges that come with securing critical healthcare infrastructure.

1.1 Overview of Medical IoT (MIoT) and Connected Healthcare Devices

Alright, let's start with the obvious: everything in healthcare is getting "smart" these days. Smart insulin pumps, smart pacemakers, smart infusion pumps, even smart hospital beds. And yet, somehow, no one seems to ask the most important question—just how "smart" is a device if a hacker can break into it with nothing more than an internet connection and a little bit of patience?

Welcome to the world of Medical IoT (MIoT), where cutting-edge technology meets cybersecurity nightmares. The same connectivity that allows doctors to monitor patients remotely is also a backdoor waiting to be exploited. And trust me, cybercriminals aren't sitting this one out. They're already infiltrating medical networks, hijacking life-saving devices, and turning hospitals into ransom notes.

If you're thinking, "That sounds terrifying,"—good! It should. Because while MIoT is revolutionizing patient care, it's also introducing security risks no one was prepared for. And that's exactly why we need to talk about it.

What Exactly Is Medical IoT?

In simple terms, Medical IoT (MIoT) refers to any internet-connected medical device. These devices collect, transmit, and store patient data, allowing doctors to monitor health conditions, adjust treatments, and even perform remote surgeries. It's an incredible advancement in medicine, but—big surprise—security was an afterthought.

Let's break it down. Medical IoT consists of three key components:

- **Smart Medical Devices** – This includes everything from wearable fitness trackers to implantable pacemakers to AI-powered diagnostic tools. If it collects data and connects to the internet, it's part of MIoT.
- **Healthcare Networks** – These are the hospital systems, cloud platforms, and remote monitoring services that make it all work. Unfortunately, they're often riddled with vulnerabilities.
- **Cloud & APIs** – Patient data doesn't just sit in a single device—it's uploaded to cloud storage, analyzed by AI, and shared through APIs. Which means that if a hacker finds one weak link, they can access an entire healthcare system.

Sounds great, right? In theory, yes. In practice? Well… let's just say hospitals aren't exactly known for having bulletproof cybersecurity.

Why the Sudden Boom in Connected Healthcare?

A decade ago, MIoT barely existed. Today, it's everywhere. What changed?

- **Aging Population & Chronic Diseases** – More people need constant health monitoring. IoT makes it possible to track vitals 24/7 without keeping patients in hospitals.
- **Telemedicine & Remote Care** – Thanks to COVID-19, remote healthcare skyrocketed. Patients expect virtual consultations, and MIoT devices make them possible.
- **Cost Savings** – Hospitals love MIoT because it reduces patient visits and lowers costs. Why keep a patient in the ICU when a smart device can monitor them at home?
- **Big Data & AI in Healthcare** – The more data we collect, the better AI can predict diseases. MIoT feeds that data, creating smarter healthcare solutions.

All of this sounds fantastic—until you realize most of these devices were designed with zero security in mind.

The Dark Side of Medical IoT: A Hacker's Playground

Here's the problem with connected healthcare: for every benefit, there's a security risk.

- **Smart insulin pumps**? Great for diabetics—terrifying if hacked. (Yes, attackers can remotely alter dosages.)
- **Internet-connected pacemakers**? Life-saving technology—until someone exploits a vulnerability and shuts it off.
- **Wearable health monitors**? Fantastic for fitness—but a privacy nightmare if your heart rate data gets leaked to advertisers (or insurance companies).

Hospital networks with unsecured IoT devices? Oh boy. Let's just say hospitals aren't just treating patients; they're treating malware infections too.

MIoT devices often suffer from:

- **Hardcoded passwords** (because why not make life easy for hackers?)
- **Unpatched firmware** (because updating devices in a hospital is apparently too much trouble).
- **Exposed APIs & weak encryption** (because security is boring and innovation is cool, right?).

The result? Hackers don't just have a way in—they have multiple ways in. And once inside, they can manipulate patient data, take control of life-critical devices, or hold an entire hospital hostage with ransomware.

Real-World MIoT Hacks That Will Keep You Up at Night

If you think all of this is theoretical, think again. Hackers are already exploiting MIoT vulnerabilities. Here are a few terrifying examples:

- **The Pacemaker Hack** – Security researchers demonstrated how easy it is to hijack a pacemaker. They showed that an attacker could remotely drain its battery, alter its pacing, or even shut it off entirely. (Yes, remotely.)
- **The Infusion Pump Attack** – Vulnerabilities in smart infusion pumps allowed researchers to adjust medication dosages. Imagine what could happen in the hands of a malicious hacker.
- **Hospital Ransomware Epidemic** – Attacks like WannaCry and NotPetya have shut down entire hospitals. Without access to their MIoT systems, hospitals

couldn't perform surgeries, access patient records, or even admit new patients. Lives were at risk—all because of poor cybersecurity.

The worst part? Most of these attacks exploited basic security flaws that could have been prevented.

The Road Ahead: Can We Fix This Mess?

So, what's the solution? Do we just rip MIoT out of hospitals and go back to clipboards and paper charts? Not exactly.

The key to securing Medical IoT lies in:

- **Stronger Authentication & Encryption** – No more hardcoded passwords or weak logins. If you can secure your Netflix account with 2FA, your pacemaker should have it too.
- **Regular Firmware Updates** – Hospitals need to treat software patches like life-saving treatments. If a device is vulnerable, fix it before hackers exploit it.
- **Stricter Compliance & Regulations** – Organizations like the FDA, HIPAA, and IEC 62304 are working to enforce better security standards. But compliance needs to move faster than hackers do.
- **Ethical Hacking & Security Research** – The best way to stop attackers? Think like one. Ethical hackers are already exposing vulnerabilities in MIoT—and companies need to start listening.

Final Thoughts: Your Smartwatch Won't Kill You (Yet)

Look, I'm not saying you should panic every time you step into a hospital. Most MIoT devices work just fine (until they don't). But the reality is, connected healthcare is evolving faster than its security—and if we don't address these risks now, we're in for a very rough future.

So, what can you do? Stay informed, stay cautious, and if you work in cybersecurity—start poking at these devices (ethically, of course). Because the only thing scarier than an unsecured MIoT device is a world where we do nothing about it.

1.2 The Growing Threat Landscape in Smart Healthcare

Let's get one thing straight—hospitals were never designed with cybersecurity in mind. They were built to save lives, not to fend off cyberattacks. But here we are, in an era where hackers can hold entire hospitals hostage with ransomware, manipulate pacemakers remotely, and steal patient data faster than a doctor can say "HIPAA violation."

The problem? Smart healthcare is expanding at breakneck speed, and security is struggling to keep up. More connected medical devices mean more entry points for hackers. More data in the cloud means more chances for leaks. More networked hospital systems mean more ways to shut down critical care. And if you think cybercriminals are going to ignore these vulnerabilities out of the goodness of their hearts, well... I have some unsecured hospital Wi-Fi to sell you.

Why Healthcare Is a Prime Target for Cyberattacks

The rise of Medical IoT (MIoT) has created a gold mine for hackers. Hospitals and medical facilities are ripe for exploitation—and here's why:

- **High-Stakes Targets** – If you hack a bank, you might steal money. If you hack a hospital, you can literally put lives at risk. That makes hospitals more willing to pay ransoms when attacked.
- **Aging Infrastructure** – Many hospitals are still running outdated operating systems (Windows XP, anyone?) and legacy devices that haven't been patched in years.
- **Massive Attack Surface** – Every smart medical device, every cloud-based EHR system, and every unsecured Wi-Fi network is another potential entry point for hackers.
- **Human Error** – Doctors and nurses aren't cybersecurity experts. Weak passwords, misplaced USB drives, and phishing emails make healthcare staff an easy target.

The result? A perfect storm of security vulnerabilities, valuable data, and high-pressure decision-making.

Top Cyber Threats Facing Smart Healthcare

The bad guys aren't just sitting around waiting for opportunities—they're actively attacking. Here are the most dangerous threats lurking in smart healthcare:

1. Ransomware: Holding Hospitals Hostage

Ransomware is the biggest nightmare in modern healthcare. Hackers encrypt hospital data, lock down critical systems, and demand payment to restore access. And when medical devices, electronic health records (EHRs), and entire hospital networks are suddenly inaccessible, people can die.

- **WannaCry (2017):** This infamous ransomware attack crippled the UK's National Health Service (NHS), shutting down hospitals, canceling surgeries, and forcing doctors to turn away patients.
- **Ryuk & Conti (2020-2022):** These ransomware groups targeted over 400 hospitals worldwide, demanding multi-million-dollar ransoms. Some hospitals had to divert emergency patients because their systems were down.

Why is ransomware so effective? Because hospitals can't afford downtime. When lives are on the line, they're more likely to pay up.

2. Data Breaches: Selling Patient Records on the Dark Web

If you thought credit card data was valuable, wait until you see how much patient records sell for on the black market. Stolen medical records contain names, Social Security numbers, insurance details, and even private medical histories—making them far more profitable than financial data.

- **Anthem Data Breach (2015):** 78.8 million patient records stolen.
- **Exposed EHR Databases (2020-2022):** Misconfigured cloud databases leaked millions of patient records—no hacking required.

The worst part? Once your health data is stolen, you can't reset it like a password.

3. Medical Device Hacking: When Your Pacemaker Gets Pwned

Modern medical devices—pacemakers, insulin pumps, MRI machines—are all connected to the internet. And if they're connected, they can be hacked.

- **Pacemaker Vulnerabilities (2017):** Researchers found that 465,000 pacemakers had security flaws that could let attackers drain the battery or alter heart rates remotely.
- **Insulin Pump Hacks:** Some models were so insecure that hackers could deliver a lethal insulin dose remotely.

- **MRI & CT Scan Manipulation**: Security flaws in imaging devices could allow attackers to alter scan results, potentially misdiagnosing patients.

Most of these attacks are preventable—but many medical devices can't be easily patched or updated, leaving them vulnerable for years.

4. API & Cloud Attacks: Where Your Health Data Gets Exposed

Hospitals love cloud computing. It makes EHRs accessible anywhere, enables telemedicine, and supports AI-powered diagnostics. But cloud services are a prime target for cyberattacks.

- **Weak API Security** – Many healthcare APIs lack proper authentication, making it easy for attackers to steal patient data.
- **Misconfigured Cloud Storage** – Hospitals frequently leave patient records exposed in unsecured cloud databases, leading to massive data breaches.
- **Third-Party Vendor Risks** – Many hospitals rely on external cloud providers, meaning one weak vendor can expose an entire system.

As more patient data moves to the cloud, attackers are shifting their focus from hospital networks to cloud vulnerabilities.

5. Phishing & Social Engineering: Hacking Humans

Let's be honest—hospital staff aren't cybersecurity pros. Doctors and nurses fall for phishing emails all the time, and hackers exploit this weakness constantly.

- **Fake IT Support Scams** – Hackers pose as "tech support" to trick staff into giving up credentials.
- **Malicious Email Attachments** – Clicking one bad link can infect an entire hospital network with ransomware.
- **Weak Passwords** – "123456" is not a secure password, yet medical staff still use them.

Even the best security systems fail if employees keep opening the door for hackers.

How Do We Fix This?

So, what's the solution? Burn it all down and go back to paper charts? Tempting, but not exactly practical. Instead, we need to take cybersecurity as seriously as patient care.

Here's what hospitals, device manufacturers, and IT teams need to do:

✓ **Implement Stronger Authentication** – No more default passwords or weak logins. Medical devices and hospital networks need multi-factor authentication (MFA) and biometric security.

✓ **Regular Security Patching** – Outdated software = hacker playground. Hospitals must update and patch systems regularly, even if it's inconvenient.

✓ **Zero Trust Architecture (ZTA)** – Hospitals should assume everything is compromised until proven otherwise. Restrict access, segment networks, and limit what devices can communicate with each other.

✓ **Better Employee Training** – Phishing attacks work because people aren't trained to spot them. Security awareness needs to be mandatory for hospital staff.

✓ **Government Regulations & Compliance** – Groups like HIPAA, FDA, and IEC 62304 need to enforce stricter security standards for medical IoT devices. No more rushed, insecure technology in hospitals.

Final Thoughts: Hackers Aren't Taking a Lunch Break

Look, cybercriminals aren't slowing down anytime soon. If anything, they're getting better at exploiting healthcare systems. Hospitals, device manufacturers, and IT teams need to wake up and start treating cybersecurity as a life-or-death issue—because in smart healthcare, it actually is.

So, if you're in the medical field, take security seriously. If you're a patient, demand better protection. And if you're a hacker (the ethical kind), start poking at these systems—before the bad guys do.

1.3 Attack Surfaces in Medical IoT Devices and Networks

Let's play a little game. Imagine you're a hacker (a nice, ethical one, of course). Your mission? Break into a hospital's Medical IoT (MIoT) system. Where do you start? The Wi-Fi? The cloud? Maybe the smart infusion pump?

The truth is, there's no shortage of entry points in a modern hospital. From unsecured medical devices to weak network configurations, the attack surface is bigger than a hospital cafeteria menu—and just as overwhelming.

Cybercriminals don't need to brute-force their way into a network when dozens of doors are already open. A poorly configured MRI machine, a nurse's stolen credentials, or even an unpatched smart thermometer could be the weak link that lets attackers waltz right in.

So, let's break it down. What are the main attack surfaces in Medical IoT? And more importantly, how can we lock them down?

1. Devices: The Weakest Link in the Chain

Medical IoT devices weren't built for security—they were built to work. The result? A massive collection of connected gadgets with poor security hygiene.

A. Unpatched & Outdated Devices

Hospitals are still using old, unsupported equipment that can't be patched or updated. Some are running software so ancient that hackers could break in with exploits from a decade ago.

◆ **Case Study**: In 2022, researchers found that over 100 models of infusion pumps had critical vulnerabilities. These pumps deliver medication to patients, meaning a hacker could alter dosages remotely.

B. Default & Hardcoded Credentials

Many medical IoT devices ship with default passwords like admin/admin. Some even have hardcoded credentials buried in the firmware. If an attacker finds these, it's game over—they can access, modify, or shut down the device entirely.

◆ **Real-World Example**: A 2019 report found that over 1,400 medical devices in U.S. hospitals were using default manufacturer passwords that hadn't been changed.

C. Lack of Encryption & Authentication

Some medical devices still transmit data in plain text (yes, in 2025). That means anyone with a basic packet sniffer can intercept sensitive patient data.

◆ **Example**: A team of security researchers demonstrated how they could intercept and alter patient vitals in real-time by exploiting a hospital's unsecured medical device protocols.

💡 **Solution:**

✓ Regular software and firmware updates.

✓ Disable default credentials & use strong authentication.

✓ Encrypt all data transmissions.

2. Networks: The Hospital's Digital Nervous System (And a Hacker's Playground)

If a medical IoT device is a single weak link, then a hospital's network is the giant web connecting all those weak links together. A single vulnerability here can give attackers access to everything.

A. Unsecured Wi-Fi & Poor Network Segmentation

Many hospitals use the same network for patient records, medical devices, and guest Wi-Fi. That's like storing gold in an unlocked drawer next to the coffee machine—it's just asking to be stolen.

◆ **Worst-Case Scenario**: A hacker connects to hospital Wi-Fi, hops over to the main network, and suddenly, they have access to life-supporting devices.

B. Poorly Configured Firewalls & Open Ports

Hospitals rely on third-party vendors for software and remote monitoring. But if these services require open ports, they create a backdoor for attackers.

◆ **Shodan Search Surprise**: Hackers (and researchers) use tools like Shodan to scan for open, exposed medical devices—many of which have no authentication at all.

💡 **Solution:**

✓ **Segment networks**—medical devices should never be on the same network as guests.

✓ Use firewalls, VPNs, and intrusion detection systems (IDS) to monitor for unauthorized access.

✓ Disable unnecessary services and open ports.

3. APIs & Cloud Services: The Invisible Attack Surface

Modern healthcare depends on cloud computing and APIs. Hospitals use cloud storage for patient data, telemedicine apps, and even AI-powered diagnostics. But with all this convenience comes a new set of risks.

A. Weak API Security

APIs (Application Programming Interfaces) allow devices and systems to communicate, but if they're not properly secured, hackers can use them to extract sensitive data.

◆ **Example**: In 2021, an unsecured API exposed millions of COVID-19 test results, allowing anyone to retrieve private health data with a simple web request.

B. Misconfigured Cloud Storage

Hospitals store enormous amounts of patient data in the cloud, but many fail to secure it properly. A single misconfigured cloud database can expose millions of records.

◆ **Example**: In 2022, a major healthcare provider accidentally left an entire cloud database of patient information exposed to the internet—no password required.

💡 **Solution:**

✓ Secure APIs with authentication and access controls.

✓ Encrypt data at rest and in transit.

✓ Conduct regular security audits of cloud configurations.

4. The Human Factor: The Biggest Security Risk of All

You can have the best security measures in place, but none of it matters if hospital staff click on phishing emails or write passwords on sticky notes.

A. Phishing & Social Engineering

Attackers don't need to hack into networks if they can trick someone into giving them access. Social engineering tactics like phishing emails, fake IT support calls, and credential stuffing are ridiculously effective.

◆ **Example**: In 2020, a ransomware attack on a hospital started with a simple phishing email. One employee clicked a malicious link, and within hours, the entire network was locked down.

B. Insider Threats

Not all threats come from outsiders. Disgruntled employees or careless staff members can leak credentials, install malware, or sell access to criminals.

◆ **Example**: In 2019, a hospital technician sold patient records on the dark web after copying them to a USB drive.

💡 Solution:

✓ Train staff to recognize phishing & social engineering attacks.

✓ Implement role-based access control (RBAC)—staff should only access what they need.

✓ Monitor employee activity for suspicious behavior.

Final Thoughts: The Attack Surface Will Keep Growing

The more we connect medical devices, the bigger the attack surface gets. Hospitals aren't just medical facilities anymore—they're digital ecosystems full of devices, networks, and cloud services. And every single connection is a potential vulnerability.

So, what's the takeaway? Hackers aren't getting dumber, and hospitals aren't getting any less connected. The only way to stay ahead is to secure every layer—devices, networks, APIs, the cloud, and yes, even the humans who keep clicking on phishing emails.

Because in a world where your pacemaker, insulin pump, and entire hospital system can be hacked, cybersecurity isn't just an IT issue—it's a matter of life and death.

1.4 Regulations and Compliance (HIPAA, FDA, IEC 62304)

Let's be honest—nobody gets excited about regulations. They're like the vegetables of cybersecurity: not the most thrilling thing on your plate, but absolutely necessary for keeping you healthy (or in this case, keeping patients and their data safe).

But here's the thing—understanding regulations isn't just about avoiding fines. It's about staying ahead of threats, ensuring patient safety, and preventing a hacker from turning someone's pacemaker into their personal experiment.

So, grab your metaphorical seatbelt, because we're diving into the world of medical IoT compliance. Buckle up—it's going to be a ride filled with acronyms, but I promise to make it worth your while.

Why Compliance in Medical IoT Matters

If a hospital gets hacked, it's not just a technical problem—it's a legal nightmare. Medical IoT devices handle life-or-death data—patient vitals, drug dosages, and even real-time monitoring of implantable devices. One security breach could mean unauthorized access to private health records or, worse, direct control over medical devices.

That's why organizations like HIPAA, the FDA, and IEC 62304 set security and safety standards for medical devices. While following them may feel like doing homework for a class you never signed up for, they serve a real purpose: protecting patient data, ensuring device reliability, and keeping hospitals from turning into hacker playgrounds.

Let's break them down, shall we?

HIPAA: The Gatekeeper of Patient Privacy

If you've ever worked in healthcare, you've heard of HIPAA (Health Insurance Portability and Accountability Act). It's basically the big, scary rulebook for how patient data should be handled, stored, and protected.

What HIPAA Covers in Medical IoT

Protected Health Information (PHI) → If it's medical data that can identify a patient (like names, medical histories, or biometric data), it must be protected.

Data Encryption → PHI should be encrypted at rest and in transit, so even if a hacker gets their hands on it, they can't read it.

Access Controls → Only authorized personnel should be able to access PHI. That means role-based access, multi-factor authentication, and strict permissions.

Incident Response → If a security breach happens, it must be reported. There are no "oops, let's pretend this didn't happen" scenarios here.

◆ **HIPAA Horror Story**: In 2019, a healthcare provider was fined $3 million because hackers stole unencrypted patient records from an unsecured FTP server. Lesson? Encrypt. Everything.

💡 **HIPAA Takeaways for Medical IoT:**

✔ Ensure end-to-end encryption of patient data.

✔ Implement strict access controls on MIoT devices.

✔ Regularly test for security vulnerabilities to prevent breaches.

FDA Regulations: Securing Medical Devices from Day One

The U.S. Food and Drug Administration (FDA) isn't just about approving new drugs—it also regulates medical IoT devices to make sure they are safe and secure before hitting the market.

Key FDA Guidelines for Medical IoT Security

Pre-Market Security Requirements → Any new medical device must include built-in cybersecurity features (i.e., strong authentication, encryption, and patchability).

Post-Market Cybersecurity Monitoring → Manufacturers must provide software updates and patches for known vulnerabilities.

Security Testing → Devices should undergo penetration testing and risk assessments before and after deployment.

Coordinated Vulnerability Disclosure → If a security flaw is discovered, manufacturers must inform hospitals and users immediately and provide a solution.

◆ **Real-World Example**: In 2017, the FDA recalled 465,000 pacemakers because they were hackable. A simple software update was needed, but guess what? Many hospitals never installed it, leaving patients vulnerable.

💡 **FDA Takeaways for Medical IoT:**

✓ Medical devices must be secure by design—security cannot be an afterthought.

✓ Patch management is critical—outdated firmware is a hacker's best friend.

✓ Hospitals should demand regular security updates from vendors.

IEC 62304: The Software Safety Standard

Now, let's talk about IEC 62304—the international standard for medical device software development. This one is all about ensuring software in medical IoT devices is built correctly and securely.

What IEC 62304 Covers

Software Lifecycle Management → Developers must follow a structured, well-documented process for medical software development.

Risk Management → Every piece of software must have a risk assessment to determine how it could fail or be exploited.

Security Updates & Maintenance → Manufacturers must have a plan for software patches and long-term security updates.

Testing & Validation → Devices must undergo thorough testing to make sure they work safely and can withstand cyber threats.

◆ **Example**: An infusion pump manufacturer failed to follow IEC 62304 standards and released software with a critical flaw that allowed unauthorized remote control of the device. The result? A nationwide recall.

💡 **IEC 62304 Takeaways for Medical IoT:**

✓ Developers must follow a strict, well-documented software development process.

✓ Regular penetration testing and code reviews are mandatory.

✓ Security doesn't stop at deployment—ongoing updates are a must.

Regulations Are Annoying, But Ignoring Them Is Worse

I get it—nobody likes regulations. They slow things down, add paperwork, and force developers to jump through compliance hoops. But the alternative? Unsecured medical devices, massive data breaches, and multi-million-dollar lawsuits.

Following HIPAA, FDA guidelines, and IEC 62304 isn't just about ticking boxes—it's about ensuring patients aren't put at risk because of lazy cybersecurity practices.

Because at the end of the day, no one wants to be the person responsible for a hospital-wide ransomware attack, a hacked pacemaker, or a medical device scandal that makes headlines. Security and compliance go hand in hand—and if you think they're annoying now, just wait until you see the consequences of ignoring them.

Now, take a deep breath—we survived the compliance talk. Let's move on to how to actually defend Medical IoT devices in the wild. 🚀

1.5 Ethical and Legal Considerations in Medical IoT Security

Let's be real—when it comes to hacking medical IoT devices, the stakes are a bit higher than your usual cybersecurity escapades. If someone hacks a smart fridge, your ice cream melts. If someone hacks a pacemaker, insulin pump, or ventilator—well, let's just say the consequences are significantly less delicious and way more life-threatening.

That's why, before we dive deeper into the world of Medical IoT (MIoT) security, we need to have a serious chat about ethics and legality. Because as much as I love breaking things in the name of security, there's a fine line between ethical hacking and cybercrime—especially when people's lives are on the line.

Hacking in Healthcare: Just Because You Can Doesn't Mean You Should

If you've been in cybersecurity long enough, you've probably asked yourself at some point:

"I wonder if I could hack this..."

And look, I get it. That curiosity is what makes good security researchers great. But when it comes to medical devices, we need to step back and think about the ethical implications of our actions.

Ask yourself:

If I exploit a vulnerability in a hospital network, could I put patients at risk?

If I publish a zero-day for a pacemaker, could someone use it maliciously before a fix is available?

If I test a device without permission, am I crossing the line from research into illegal activity?

The bottom line? Medical IoT security isn't just about finding vulnerabilities—it's about fixing them without harming people in the process.

Let's break down the ethical and legal side of MIoT security.

Ethical Hacking vs. Criminal Hacking: Where's the Line?

Ethical hacking is all about identifying vulnerabilities before the bad guys do. But what separates ethical security research from cybercrime?

◆ Ethical Hacking in MIoT:

✔ Conducting authorized security testing on medical devices.

✔ Working responsibly with manufacturers to fix vulnerabilities.

✔ Reporting security flaws through coordinated disclosure programs.

✔ Ensuring that security research doesn't put patients at risk.

✖ Unethical (or Illegal) Hacking in MIoT:

⊘ Hacking without permission, even if you have good intentions.

⊘ Exploiting vulnerabilities for personal gain or malicious intent.

⊘ Disclosing security flaws in live medical devices before a patch is available.

⊘ Running penetration tests on hospital networks without explicit authorization.

Here's the kicker—intent doesn't matter when it comes to the law. Even if you're just "testing" a hospital's network to prove a point, you could still face serious legal consequences.

Legal Frameworks Governing Medical IoT Security

So, what laws regulate Medical IoT hacking? Well, there are quite a few, and they're not exactly hacker-friendly.

1. The Computer Fraud and Abuse Act (CFAA) (U.S.)

The CFAA is basically the "Do Not Hack Without Permission" law. It makes it illegal to:

Access a computer or network without authorization.

Exceed authorized access (even if you technically have login credentials).

Interfere with medical systems or data.

⚠ Why It Matters for MIoT:

If you hack a hospital's network without permission, expect handcuffs, not a bug bounty.

If you exploit a medical device vulnerability irresponsibly, you could be charged with a federal crime.

2. HIPAA & Patient Privacy Laws

Remember HIPAA? The Health Insurance Portability and Accountability Act isn't just about doctors—it also covers medical IoT security.

HIPAA violations can happen if a hacker:

Exposes or steals patient health data (PHI).

Modifies medical records (imagine changing someone's allergy info—yikes).

Disrupts hospital systems that store patient data.

🏛 **Penalty**? Fines up to $1.5 million per violation. Yes, you read that right—per violation.

3. The DMCA & Medical Device Firmware

The Digital Millennium Copyright Act (DMCA) was meant to prevent software piracy, but it also applies to medical device hacking.

💻 **Under the DMCA, it's illegal to:**

Reverse-engineer proprietary medical device firmware.

Circumvent software locks or encryption on medical IoT devices.

Modify a medical device's code without manufacturer permission.

⚠ **But There's a Loophole!**

Security researchers can legally analyze medical devices under the DMCA exemption for security testing—but only if they:

Own the device (i.e., you can hack your own pacemaker, but not someone else's).

Conduct research in a controlled environment (not in a hospital).

Act in good faith (no selling exploits to black hat forums).

The Ethical Path: Coordinated Disclosure & Responsible Research

So, what should an ethical MIoT hacker do if they find a vulnerability?

◆ Step 1: Contact the Manufacturer

Find the right security team or responsible disclosure program.

Provide detailed evidence of the vulnerability (but don't exploit it on live systems!).

Give them reasonable time to fix it before going public.

◆ Step 2: Work with Regulatory Bodies

If a manufacturer ignores your report, contact the FDA, CERT, or a healthcare cybersecurity agency.

In extreme cases, work with ethical hacking organizations to push for fixes.

◆ Step 3: Public Disclosure (Only After a Fix Exists)

If a company patches the flaw, share your research responsibly.

Never drop a zero-day on a live system—that's a fast track to a lawsuit.

Final Thoughts: Hackers vs. Healthcare—The Right Way to Do It

Look, I get it—hacking MIoT devices is a fascinating challenge. But unlike breaking into a smart thermostat, medical IoT security has real-life consequences.

A single vulnerability could:

💀 Put lives at risk.
⚕ Shut down an entire hospital's network.
💰 Result in millions of dollars in fines and lawsuits.

So, if you're in this field, be the kind of hacker who protects people, not puts them in danger. Work ethically, follow the law, and help make Medical IoT safer for everyone.

Because at the end of the day, cybersecurity isn't just about breaking things—it's about making sure the right things don't break.

Chapter 2: Understanding Medical IoT Architectures

Picture this: You're in a hospital, and suddenly, every machine starts beeping wildly. A hacker has just triggered every alarm system remotely because, surprise, surprise—the devices are all connected but barely secured. From wearables to ventilators, everything in modern healthcare talks to something else, usually over insecure networks. It's like a giant, high-stakes game of telephone, but instead of a silly message getting garbled, it's patient data... or someone's heart rate.

Medical IoT architecture consists of a complex ecosystem of connected devices, networks, communication protocols, and cloud services. Understanding this architecture is essential for identifying security weaknesses and ensuring robust protection against cyber threats. This chapter breaks down the key components of MIoT, including how medical devices communicate using standards like DICOM, HL7, and MQTT, and the security challenges associated with cloud integration, remote access, and legacy systems in healthcare environments.

2.1 Components of a Medical IoT Ecosystem (Devices, Cloud, Network)

Ever wonder what happens when you strap the Internet to a stethoscope, give a hospital bed an IP address, or let a pacemaker chat with the cloud? Welcome to the Medical IoT (MIoT) ecosystem—where lifesaving devices and cutting-edge tech meet a whole lot of security risks.

In this chapter, we're going to break down the core components of Medical IoT—the devices, the cloud infrastructure, and the networks that keep everything connected. Think of it like anatomy class, but instead of dissecting frogs, we're dissecting how smart healthcare works (and how hackers might break it).

The Three Pillars of Medical IoT

Medical IoT isn't just about a single device. It's an ecosystem, made up of three major components:

Devices – Wearables, sensors, medical implants, smart hospital equipment.

Cloud – The massive infrastructure that stores, processes, and transmits patient data.

Network – The wireless and wired connections that keep everything talking to each other.

Each of these layers plays a critical role in modern healthcare, and (spoiler alert) each one has security vulnerabilities that attackers love to exploit.

Medical IoT Devices: The Gadgets Keeping Us Alive

First up, the devices—the frontline warriors of smart healthcare. These range from patient-worn wearables to surgically implanted life-supporting devices.

Types of Medical IoT Devices

◆ Wearable Health Devices

Smartwatches and fitness trackers (Apple Watch, Fitbit, Garmin).

Continuous glucose monitors (Dexcom, FreeStyle Libre).

ECG and blood pressure monitors.

◆ Implantable Medical Devices (IMDs)

Pacemakers and defibrillators.

Insulin pumps.

Neurostimulators.

◆ Hospital Equipment and Smart Medical Systems

Internet-connected infusion pumps.

MRI and CT scan machines.

Smart hospital beds and automated medication dispensers.

These devices monitor, diagnose, and even treat patients in real time. Sounds great, right? Well, here's the catch—most of them were not built with security in mind. Many still use default passwords, outdated encryption, or even plain-text communication (seriously, who thought that was a good idea?).

The Cloud: Storing and Processing Your Vital Signs

In the old days, hospitals stored patient records in file cabinets. Now, thanks to cloud computing, medical data is stored in data centers, AI-driven analytics platforms, and remote-access servers.

Key Components of Medical IoT Cloud Systems

☁ **Electronic Health Records (EHRs)** – Systems like Epic, Cerner, and MEDITECH store patient histories, test results, and prescriptions.

☁ **Remote Patient Monitoring (RPM)** – Cloud-based apps that allow doctors to check patient vitals in real time.

☁ **Telemedicine Platforms** – Video consultations, diagnostic AI, and cloud-hosted medical services.

☁ **AI-Powered Diagnostics** – Machine learning algorithms that analyze X-rays, MRIs, and genetic data to detect diseases faster than doctors.

Cloud integration makes healthcare faster, smarter, and more efficient, but it also creates massive security risks:

🏛 **Data breaches** – If cloud security is weak, millions of patient records can be leaked (think of the Anthem and WannaCry ransomware attacks).

🏛 **API vulnerabilities** – Many MIoT devices communicate with the cloud via APIs, and if those APIs are weak, attackers can manipulate medical data.

🏛 **Misconfigured storage** – Hospitals often leave unprotected databases open to the internet (yes, this happens more than you think).

The Network: How Medical IoT Devices "Talk"

Finally, let's talk about networks—the highways that connect Medical IoT devices to each other and the cloud.

Types of MIoT Networks

☠ **Wi-Fi (802.11)** – Used in hospitals and clinics, but often insecure if not properly configured.

☠ **Bluetooth & BLE (Low Energy)** – Found in wearables and implants (fun fact: pacemakers can be hacked via Bluetooth).

☠ **Zigbee & Z-Wave** – Low-power wireless networks used in smart hospitals.

☠ **NFC (Near Field Communication)** – Used in contactless payments and medication tracking.

☠ **Cellular (4G, 5G, LTE-M)** – Powers remote patient monitoring and emergency telemedicine.

☠ **Proprietary medical networks** – Some hospitals use closed networks, but those aren't always as secure as they seem.

Security Risks Across the Ecosystem

Now that we know the core components of Medical IoT, let's look at where things can go horribly wrong.

Common Security Vulnerabilities

💀 **Hardcoded Credentials** – Many medical devices ship with default usernames and passwords (and hospitals often don't change them).

💀 **Unencrypted Data Transmission** – Some MIoT devices send patient data in plaintext (seriously, why?).

💀 **Unpatched Firmware** – Hospitals aren't great at updating old medical devices, leaving them vulnerable to zero-day exploits.

☠ **Weak API Security** – If an attacker hijacks a cloud API, they can manipulate medical records or shut down life-supporting devices.

☠ **Physical Access Attacks** – If a hacker can get physical access to a device, they can dump its firmware, extract sensitive data, or inject malware.

Final Thoughts: The Good, the Bad, and the Hackable

Medical IoT is an incredible leap forward in healthcare. It saves lives, improves diagnostics, and makes Star Trek-level medicine a reality.

But—and this is a BIG but—it also comes with serious security challenges.

Hospitals are notoriously bad at keeping their tech up to date, and many medical devices are shockingly easy to hack. That's why security professionals (like you and me) need to step up and lock down the MIoT ecosystem before the bad guys do.

In the next sections, we'll dive deeper into attack strategies, vulnerabilities, and real-world exploits. But for now, just remember: if your pacemaker has Wi-Fi, you better hope it doesn't have a default password like "1234".

2.2 Medical Device Communication Protocols (DICOM, HL7, MQTT)

Imagine you walk into a hospital, get an MRI scan, and moments later, your doctor pulls up the images on their tablet. Magic? Nope. It's all thanks to medical device communication protocols—the secret sauce that allows medical IoT (MIoT) devices, hospital systems, and cloud platforms to talk to each other.

Now, imagine what happens if these protocols aren't secured properly (spoiler alert: chaos). Unencrypted data, weak authentication, and outdated standards can turn a life-saving technology into a hacker's playground. In this section, we'll break down three major protocols—DICOM, HL7, and MQTT—and the security risks that come with them.

The Language of Medical Devices

Medical IoT devices don't just work in isolation. They rely on standardized communication protocols to exchange patient data, imaging files, and real-time health metrics. Here are the three big ones:

DICOM (Digital Imaging and Communications in Medicine) – Used for medical images (X-rays, MRIs, CT scans).

HL7 (Health Level Seven) – Handles electronic health records (EHRs) and patient data exchange.

MQTT (Message Queuing Telemetry Transport) – A lightweight IoT protocol used for real-time monitoring and telemedicine.

Each of these protocols is essential for modern healthcare—but they also come with security weaknesses that attackers love to exploit.

DICOM: The Backbone of Medical Imaging

Ever wondered how an MRI machine talks to a hospital's database? That's DICOM in action. DICOM is the global standard for handling, storing, and transmitting medical images and related data. If you've ever had an X-ray or ultrasound, chances are your images were processed via DICOM.

How DICOM Works

☐ Medical imaging device (MRI, CT, X-ray) captures images.
🔖 DICOM protocol transmits the images to a PACS (Picture Archiving and Communication System).
☐☐ Doctors access and analyze images from workstations or cloud-based platforms.

Security Issues in DICOM

🔒 **Unencrypted Image Transfers** – Many hospitals still send DICOM images over plaintext (yes, even sensitive patient scans).
🔑 **Weak Authentication** – Some DICOM systems rely on basic username-password authentication, making them easy to brute-force.
☠ **Exposed PACS Servers** – Hackers can scan the internet (via Shodan) and find exposed medical image databases (this has actually happened).

Fun fact (or nightmare fuel): In 2019, security researchers found millions of unprotected X-rays, MRIs, and CT scans exposed online due to misconfigured DICOM servers. Imagine your broken leg X-ray floating around the dark web.

Security Fixes:

✓ Enable encryption (TLS) for DICOM transfers.

✓ Enforce strong authentication and access controls.

✓ Never expose PACS servers to the public internet (seriously, why is this still happening?).

HL7: The Language of Patient Data

Let's talk about HL7 (Health Level Seven)—the protocol that allows hospitals, clinics, and labs to exchange electronic health records (EHRs) seamlessly.

What HL7 Does

🖫 Transfers patient records between different hospital systems (e.g., lab reports, prescriptions, admission data).
🏛 Ensures interoperability between different healthcare software vendors.
💬 Acts like a translator between different hospital databases and applications.

Security Issues in HL7

🚫 **No Built-in Security** – HL7 was not designed with encryption or authentication in mind (because why secure patient data, right?).
🐛 **Plaintext Communication** – Many hospitals still send HL7 messages over unencrypted channels.
⚠️ **Man-in-the-Middle (MITM) Attacks** – Attackers can intercept and modify HL7 messages (imagine a hacker changing a patient's blood type).

Security Fixes:

✓ Use secure HL7 over TLS (HL7 v3 supports encryption, but many hospitals still use HL7 v2).

✓ Implement access controls to restrict unauthorized data access.

✓ Monitor HL7 traffic for anomalies (e.g., unusual data modifications).

Fun fact: Hackers have demonstrated MITM attacks on HL7 traffic, showing that they could alter medication dosages in hospital records. Imagine a dose of 10mg getting changed to 100mg—not exactly the kind of upgrade you want.

MQTT: The IoT Protocol Keeping Patients Connected

Now, let's talk about MQTT (Message Queuing Telemetry Transport)—the lightweight IoT protocol that powers remote patient monitoring, smart medical devices, and real-time alerts.

How MQTT Works in Healthcare

⊕ Wearable sensors (heart rate monitors, glucose meters) send data to an MQTT broker.
🕊 The broker relays this data to cloud platforms and hospital dashboards.
☐☐ Doctors and AI systems analyze real-time patient vitals.

Security Issues in MQTT

☠ **No Built-in Encryption** – MQTT by default does not encrypt messages (yes, even patient vitals).
🔓 **Weak Authentication** – Many hospitals use default MQTT credentials (e.g., admin:admin—yes, really).
🕊 **Susceptible to Packet Sniffing** – Attackers can intercept unencrypted MQTT messages and modify them.

Security Fixes:

✓ Use MQTT over TLS (secure encryption for message transport).

✓ Enable authentication (use strong passwords, API keys, or OAuth for MQTT brokers).

✓ Monitor for unusual MQTT traffic patterns (e.g., sudden spikes in data transmission could indicate an attack).

Final Thoughts: The Good, the Bad, and the (Hackable) Ugly

Medical IoT devices need communication protocols to function, but many of these protocols were not designed with security in mind.

We just saw how:

✓ DICOM helps process medical images but can expose millions of scans if misconfigured.

✓ **HL7 makes patient data portable but has no built-in encryption (yikes!).

✓ MQTT powers real-time health monitoring but is often left wide open to attacks.

The good news? Security measures exist to fix these issues. The bad news? Many hospitals still aren't using them.

If you take one thing away from this chapter, let it be this:

🚨 If you ever get an MRI, just pray your hospital's DICOM server isn't on Shodan. 🚨

2.3 Wireless Technologies in Healthcare: Bluetooth, Zigbee, Wi-Fi, NFC

Alright, let's talk about wireless technologies in healthcare—because nothing screams futuristic hospital like a bunch of beeping devices, smart wearables, and wireless patient monitoring systems. Gone are the days of clunky wired machines; today, we have Bluetooth-enabled insulin pumps, Zigbee-based nurse call systems, Wi-Fi-powered telemedicine, and NFC for contactless medical transactions.

Sounds great, right? Well… here's the catch. The same technologies that make healthcare more efficient also make it more hackable. We're talking about unsecured Bluetooth connections, Wi-Fi eavesdropping, Zigbee jamming, and NFC cloning—all potentially life-threatening in a medical environment. So, let's break down these wireless wonders (and nightmares).

Bluetooth: The Convenience & The Chaos

Bluetooth is everywhere in healthcare—glucose monitors, smart prosthetics, fitness trackers, heart rate monitors, and even surgical tools. It's a low-power, short-range wireless technology that allows medical devices to communicate without wires.

How Bluetooth Works in Healthcare

📡 A smart insulin pump sends data to a patient's phone.

✚ A doctor wirelessly adjusts a pacemaker's settings.

☺ A smartwatch detects irregular heartbeats and alerts emergency services.

Security Issues in Bluetooth

💀 **Default & Weak Pairing** – Many medical devices use default or weak pairing codes (e.g., 0000, 1234).

📡 **Eavesdropping & Sniffing** – Attackers can capture unencrypted Bluetooth traffic using cheap hardware.

🔒 **MITM Attacks** – Without proper encryption, hackers can perform Man-in-the-Middle attacks and alter medical data.

Real-World Scare: Researchers have demonstrated hacking Bluetooth pacemakers, proving that an attacker could remotely alter heart rhythms (which is as terrifying as it sounds).

Security Fixes:

✓ Use Bluetooth Low Energy (BLE) with Secure Connections Mode.

✓ Implement proper encryption (AES-128 for BLE).

✓ Disable Bluetooth when not in use (simple, but effective).

Zigbee: The Silent Threat to Smart Hospitals

Zigbee is the go-to wireless protocol for low-power medical IoT (MIoT) devices, including nurse call systems, patient tracking tags, and hospital lighting automation. It's an alternative to Wi-Fi that allows devices to communicate in a mesh network—but it comes with security risks.

How Zigbee Works in Healthcare

✚ Hospital sensors monitor room temperatures and air quality.

☎ Nurse call buttons send alerts wirelessly.

📡 Smart infusion pumps wirelessly transmit patient data.

Security Issues in Zigbee

💀 **Lack of Encryption by Default** – Zigbee devices often transmit data unencrypted (why?!).

📡 **Easy Signal Jamming** – A simple radio interference attack can disable a hospital's Zigbee-powered emergency alert system.

🔒 **Key Capture Attacks** – Attackers can extract network encryption keys and take control of smart hospital devices.

Real-World Scare: Researchers have hacked Zigbee-based smart lighting in hospitals, proving that attackers could remotely turn off critical lights in an operating room (imagine performing surgery in pitch darkness).

Security Fixes:

✓ Enable AES-128 encryption for Zigbee communication.

✓ Use Zigbee 3.0 with secure key exchange.

✓ Deploy intrusion detection to spot unauthorized Zigbee traffic.

Wi-Fi: The Backbone of Connected Healthcare

Wi-Fi is the king of wireless networking in hospitals, powering everything from electronic health record (EHR) systems to patient monitoring and telemedicine. But with great power comes great attack surfaces.

How Wi-Fi Works in Healthcare

📡 Doctors access patient records wirelessly on tablets.

☐ Wireless infusion pumps communicate with cloud servers.

✚ Patients use hospital Wi-Fi for internet access.

Security Issues in Wi-Fi

☠ **Weak Passwords** – Many hospitals still use default router passwords (e.g., admin:admin).

☠ **Evil Twin Attacks** – Hackers set up fake hospital Wi-Fi networks to steal login credentials.

🔒 **Rogue Access Points** – Unauthorized Wi-Fi devices create backdoors into hospital networks.

Real-World Scare: In 2020, security researchers found thousands of unsecured hospital Wi-Fi networks, making it trivially easy for attackers to intercept patient data.

Security Fixes:

✓ Use WPA3 encryption and strong passwords.

✓ Disable WPS (Wi-Fi Protected Setup) to prevent brute-force attacks.

✓ Regularly audit Wi-Fi networks for rogue access points.

NFC: The Future of Contactless Medical Transactions

Near Field Communication (NFC) is used for secure, short-range data exchange—think contactless payments, patient ID cards, and electronic prescriptions. It's fast, convenient, and secure—until someone clones your hospital ID badge.

How NFC Works in Healthcare

▬ Doctors tap ID badges to access patient records.
✚ Patients pay hospital bills via contactless NFC payments.
🔏 Pharmacists verify prescriptions using NFC-enabled systems.

Security Issues in NFC

☠ **NFC Cloning Attacks** – Hackers can clone NFC-based hospital ID cards.

☠ **Data Interception** – Without encryption, NFC transactions can be intercepted using simple radio scanners.

🔒 **Relay Attacks** – Attackers can relay NFC signals over long distances, tricking systems into accepting fake credentials.

Real-World Scare: Security experts have demonstrated cloning NFC hospital badges in under 30 seconds, giving attackers unauthorized access to restricted medical areas.

Security Fixes:

✔ Use encryption for NFC transactions.

✔ Enable mutual authentication for NFC-based access control.

✔ Use short-range NFC antennas to limit attack range.

Final Thoughts: Wireless Healthcare is Amazing… and Terrifying

Wireless technologies have revolutionized healthcare, making it more efficient, accessible, and connected. But as we've seen:

✅ **Bluetooth makes medical devices smarter**—but can be hacked remotely.

✅ **Zigbee connects smart hospitals**—but can be jammed or intercepted.

✅ **Wi-Fi powers everything**—but remains a prime target for cyberattacks.

✅ **NFC enables secure transactions**—but can be cloned if not protected.

The bottom line? Wireless healthcare is awesome—but only if we secure it properly. Otherwise, that "smart" pacemaker might just get a little too smart for its own good. 🔐

2.4 Cloud Integration and Remote Access in Smart Healthcare

Ah, the cloud—the magical place where all our data goes to float around in cyberspace until we need it. Or, if you're a hacker, until you decide to take it. Healthcare, like everything else, has embraced cloud technology with open arms, promising instant access to patient records, real-time monitoring, and remote diagnostics. Sounds fantastic, right? Well, sure—until you realize that a single misconfigured database can expose millions of medical records to the world (oops).

Welcome to cloud-integrated smart healthcare, where your doctor can check your heart rate from their phone, your hospital can store patient records on remote servers, and cybercriminals can—well, you get the point. Let's take a deep dive into how the cloud powers healthcare and the massive security risks that come with it.

The Role of Cloud in Smart Healthcare

Cloud computing has transformed healthcare by enabling real-time data access, scalable storage, and remote collaboration. Hospitals, clinics, and even individual practitioners use cloud-based systems to:

⊕ Store and retrieve patient records (Electronic Health Records - EHRs)

📡 Enable telemedicine and remote diagnostics

☐ Monitor patients in real-time with IoT-enabled devices

🔖 Improve collaboration between doctors, pharmacies, and labs

Instead of relying on on-premise servers, healthcare organizations now outsource data storage to cloud providers like AWS, Microsoft Azure, and Google Cloud. While this brings speed, efficiency, and cost savings, it also introduces new attack vectors.

Common Cloud Security Risks in Healthcare

1. Misconfigured Cloud Storage (a.k.a. "The Digital Oops")

The number one cause of healthcare data leaks isn't some elite hacker—it's human error. A misconfigured Amazon S3 bucket or unprotected database can expose millions of patient records to anyone with an internet connection.

🏛 **Real-World Disaster**: In 2019, 2.7 million medical records were exposed due to an unsecured cloud database, leaking names, diagnoses, and payment details (yikes).

🔒 **Security Fix:**

✓ Use encryption for stored data (AES-256).

✓ Audit cloud configurations regularly.

✓ Implement strict access controls with multi-factor authentication (MFA).

2. Insecure APIs in Telemedicine & EHRs

APIs (Application Programming Interfaces) allow different healthcare applications to communicate and share data—but if not secured properly, they can be a hacker's dream come true.

📡 **Example**: A vulnerable API in a telemedicine app could allow attackers to:

✓ Hijack patient sessions

✓ Steal personal health information (PHI)

✓ Manipulate medical records

📖 **Real-World Disaster**: In 2021, researchers found vulnerabilities in major telemedicine APIs, allowing attackers to intercept doctor-patient video calls and modify prescriptions.

🔒 **Security Fix:**

✓ Implement OAuth 2.0 for secure API authentication.

✓ Use rate limiting to prevent brute-force attacks.

✓ Encrypt API communication with TLS 1.2+.

3. Remote Access Exploits: When Hackers "Log in as Doctor"

Doctors and medical staff love remote access—it allows them to review patient files from home, update prescriptions on the go, and even perform remote surgeries (yes, that's a thing now). But here's the problem: so do hackers.

If remote access systems (like RDP, VPNs, and cloud portals) aren't secured properly, attackers can:

✓ Gain full admin access to hospital systems

✓ Lock critical patient data with ransomware

✓ Intercept real-time medical device communications

📖 **Real-World Disaster**: In 2020, a hospital's remote access portal was hacked, allowing attackers to deploy ransomware that shut down critical systems—forcing ambulances to be rerouted and delaying patient care.

🔒 **Security Fix:**

✓ Require multi-factor authentication (MFA) for remote access.

✓ Use zero-trust security models—never assume any user is safe.

✓ Implement network segmentation to isolate cloud-based systems from core hospital infrastructure.

Cloud-Based Patient Monitoring: Life-Saving & Hackable

Cloud integration allows remote patient monitoring (RPM), where wearables, smart implants, and connected medical devices continuously send data to the cloud.

📢 Example:

A smart insulin pump reports glucose levels to a cloud platform.

A pacemaker uploads heart rate data for a cardiologist to review remotely.

A COVID-19 monitoring app tracks oxygen levels and alerts doctors if they drop dangerously low.

📢 The Problem?

These devices transmit sensitive patient data over wireless networks and the cloud—which means hackers can intercept or manipulate the data.

🔒 Security Fix:

✓ Use end-to-end encryption between medical IoT devices and cloud servers.

✓ Implement device authentication to prevent unauthorized access.

✓ Store only necessary health data, and delete old records regularly.

The Future: AI, Blockchain & Zero-Trust Security

As healthcare moves further into cloud-based systems, security must evolve. AI-powered threat detection, blockchain for data integrity, and zero-trust security models will help secure the future of cloud-integrated healthcare.

✅ AI-powered security tools can detect anomalous activity in cloud networks.

✓ Blockchain technology ensures tamper-proof patient records.

✓ Zero-trust security assumes every device and user is a potential threat, requiring continuous verification.

Final Thoughts: The Cloud is Great… If Secured Properly

Cloud integration has revolutionized healthcare, making it more efficient, scalable, and accessible. But with convenience comes risk—a single misconfigured cloud database, weak API, or compromised remote access can lead to catastrophic security breaches.

If done right, cloud-powered healthcare can improve patient care, streamline hospital operations, and even enable remote surgeries (yes, robotic surgeons are a thing). But if done wrong… well, let's just say you don't want your medical records up for sale on the dark web.

So, healthcare IT teams, secure your cloud—because no one wants their X-rays, prescriptions, or heart rate data floating around in cyberspace for the wrong eyes to see. 🚀

2.5 Security Challenges in Legacy and Proprietary Medical Systems

Ah, legacy systems—those ancient, creaky machines still running in hospitals like digital fossils from a bygone era. You'd think that in a world where we have AI-powered diagnostics and robotic surgeries, we wouldn't still be relying on Windows XP to run critical life-support systems (yes, really). But here we are.

And let's not forget proprietary medical systems. These black-box, vendor-locked nightmares come with zero transparency, minimal security updates, and a hefty price tag. If you thought dealing with hospital billing was bad, try convincing a medical device manufacturer to give you a patch for a decade-old ventilator (spoiler: they won't).

Let's dig into why legacy and proprietary systems refuse to die, how they create massive security risks, and what we can do to fix this mess.

Why Are Hospitals Still Using Legacy Systems?

Hospitals aren't holding onto old technology for nostalgia's sake. There are real reasons why legacy systems refuse to go away, including:

1. Cost (a.k.a. "If It Ain't Broke, We're Not Replacing It")

Medical equipment isn't like a smartphone you can upgrade every few years. A single MRI machine can cost millions of dollars, and replacing it just to upgrade the software? Yeah, not happening.

2. Certification Hassles

Regulatory approval for new medical devices (FDA, IEC 62304, HIPAA) is a slow, painful process. Hospitals prefer sticking with what works rather than navigating the bureaucratic nightmare of getting approval for a system upgrade.

3. Compatibility Issues

A hospital's entire network of devices, software, and databases is a delicate ecosystem. Updating one system might break compatibility with older machines, leading to costly downtimes and frustrated doctors screaming at IT staff.

4. Vendor Lock-in

Many medical device manufacturers use proprietary software and hardware, making it nearly impossible to upgrade without their permission (which usually comes at ridiculous costs).

Security Nightmares of Legacy Systems

Still using Windows 7 or XP in a hospital setting? You're not alone—but you're also a giant target for cybercriminals. Legacy systems come with glaring security flaws, such as:

1. Lack of Security Updates

Microsoft stopped supporting Windows XP in 2014, yet thousands of hospitals still use it.

Unpatched vulnerabilities make it trivial for hackers to deploy malware or ransomware.

🚨 Real-World Disaster:

Remember WannaCry (2017)? That ransomware attack crippled UK hospitals, delayed surgeries, and forced medical staff to record patient data with pen and paper. The root cause? Unpatched Windows XP machines.

🔒 Security Fix:

✓ Use network segmentation to isolate legacy systems.

✓ Virtualize old operating systems within protected environments.

✓ Push for vendor-supported security patches (if available).

2. Hardcoded Credentials & Weak Authentication

Many older medical devices have hardcoded admin passwords (which, surprise, are often leaked online).

Some systems don't support multi-factor authentication (MFA), making brute-force attacks ridiculously easy.

💀 Real-World Disaster:

In 2021, researchers found hardcoded passwords in widely used infusion pumps, allowing unauthorized access to medication dosages (not great).

🔒 Security Fix:

✓ Remove default or hardcoded credentials where possible.

✓ Implement network-level authentication and zero-trust security.

✓ Replace legacy systems as soon as budgets allow.

3. Lack of Encryption

Many legacy medical systems don't encrypt data in transit or at rest.

Patient data is often transmitted in plain text, making interception easy.

💀 Real-World Disaster:

A 2019 study found that over 80% of legacy medical systems fail basic encryption standards, exposing millions of patient records to potential theft.

🔒 Security Fix:

✓ Implement TLS encryption for network communications.

✓ Use full-disk encryption for legacy data storage.

✓ Migrate patient records to secure cloud-based systems when possible.

The Proprietary Software Problem: Closed-Source = Closed Security

Many medical devices run on proprietary software, meaning only the manufacturer has access to security patches and updates. This creates several problems:

1. Lack of Transparency

Hospitals can't inspect the code for vulnerabilities.

Security researchers can't legally test for weaknesses (thanks, DMCA).

2. No Third-Party Patching

If a vendor stops supporting a device, hospitals are stuck with unpatched software.

Some vendors refuse to provide security updates unless hospitals pay extra.

🚨 Real-World Disaster:

A major MRI machine vendor was caught charging hospitals thousands of dollars for basic security patches—patches that should have been free.

🔒 Security Fix:

✓ Push for open-source security models in medical software.

✓ Pressure vendors for long-term security support.

✓ Advocate for right-to-repair legislation in medical technology.

Mitigating Risks: How to Secure Legacy & Proprietary Systems

So, what can hospitals realistically do when faced with outdated, insecure systems?

1. Segment Legacy Systems from the Main Network

Keep older devices isolated to prevent lateral movement.

Use firewalls and intrusion detection systems (IDS) to monitor activity.

2. Virtualize When Possible

Run legacy systems within virtualized, sandboxed environments.

Use read-only snapshots to prevent malware persistence.

3. Implement Multi-Factor Authentication (MFA)

Even if legacy software doesn't support MFA, use network-level MFA for access.

4. Demand Vendor Support & Transparency

Push manufacturers to provide security patches beyond end-of-life.

Support open-source security initiatives in medical IoT.

Final Thoughts: Old Tech, Big Risks, Hard Choices

Legacy and proprietary systems are a ticking time bomb in healthcare cybersecurity. They remain too expensive to replace, too complex to upgrade, and too vulnerable to ignore. Hospitals are stuck between a rock and a hard place—either risk cyberattacks on outdated systems or fork over millions to replace them.

But here's the thing: attackers don't care if upgrading is expensive. They will exploit every weakness, every unpatched vulnerability, and every misconfigured system they find.

So, if you're a hospital IT administrator, start fighting for those security upgrades. If you're a cybersecurity researcher, keep exposing the flaws. And if you're a medical device manufacturer, well—maybe don't charge hospitals thousands of dollars just to patch a security bug. Just a thought. 💀

Chapter 3: Reconnaissance and Attack Surface Mapping

You wouldn't break into a bank without casing the joint first, right? (Not that I'm suggesting you rob banks—let's keep this hypothetical.) Well, hacking works the same way. Before launching an attack, a smart hacker gathers intel, identifies weak points, and maps out every possible entry. And guess what? Hospitals are filled with poorly secured devices broadcasting their presence like neon signs saying, "Hack me, please!"

This chapter covers reconnaissance techniques used to identify and map the attack surface of medical IoT systems. Topics include passive and active network scanning, using tools like Shodan and Censys to locate exposed healthcare devices, and fingerprinting firmware and software for vulnerabilities. Understanding these methods is crucial for both attackers and defenders—because the best way to secure a system is to think like someone trying to break into it.

3.1 Identifying and Enumerating Medical IoT Devices

Alright, let's play a little game called "Spot the Medical IoT Device Before It Spots You." Hospitals are filled with high-tech gadgets that beep, blink, and—when hacked—can wreak absolute havoc. But before we can talk about securing or attacking these devices, we need to find them.

That's easier said than done. Unlike your friendly neighborhood Wi-Fi router, most medical IoT (MIoT) devices aren't broadcasting a "Hack Me" SSID. They're buried deep in hospital networks, running on hidden VLANs, obscure protocols, and proprietary firmware. Some are wired, some wireless, some running ancient Windows XP, and others using custom embedded systems no one's documented in a decade.

So, how do we track down these elusive devices? Simple: we think like a hacker.

Why Device Identification Matters

Before we start scanning networks like a cyberpunk vigilante, let's talk about why identifying MIoT devices is critical:

Security Audits: You can't secure what you don't know exists. Many hospitals have shadow IT devices lurking in their networks, completely unmanaged.

Regulatory Compliance: HIPAA, FDA, and IEC 62304 all demand some level of device inventory management.

Incident Response: When something goes wrong (and trust me, it will), you need to know which device got owned before patients start getting mystery overdoses.

Pentesting & Red Teaming: If you're an ethical hacker, your job starts with mapping the attack surface before attempting any exploits.

Step 1: Passive Discovery – Listening Before Probing

The golden rule of hacking: Don't make noise if you don't have to.

Passive discovery is about observing the network rather than interacting with it directly. This approach is useful in medical environments where aggressive scanning can crash fragile devices (yes, that's a thing).

Tools for Passive Discovery

Wireshark: The go-to tool for packet sniffing. Great for capturing device traffic, MAC addresses, and protocol information.

Rogue Access Point Detection: Some medical IoT devices connect to rogue Wi-Fi networks, exposing patient data. Tools like Kismet can detect these.

NetFlow & Network Monitoring Tools: Platforms like SolarWinds, PRTG, or Splunk help passively log medical device traffic patterns.

📷 Pro Tip:

Look for DICOM (Digital Imaging and Communications in Medicine) and HL7 packets. These often lead directly to MRI machines, PACS servers, and EHR systems.

Step 2: Active Scanning – Time to Get Our Hands Dirty

Once we have a passive map of the network, it's time to get a little aggressive (but not too aggressive, unless you enjoy explaining why the ICU is offline).

Tools for Active Scanning

Nmap: The Swiss Army knife of network scanning. Use OS detection (-O) and service scanning (-sV) to fingerprint medical devices.

Masscan: If you need to scan entire hospital subnets at lightning speed.

Shodan & Censys: Check if any hospital devices are exposed to the internet (yes, this happens way more than you'd think).

SNMP Walk: Many MIoT devices use Simple Network Management Protocol. Running an snmpwalk command can reveal device names, uptime, and system details.

🔐 Pro Tip:

If you see devices running Telnet or FTP, congratulations—you've found a hacker's dream come true.

Step 3: Device Fingerprinting – What Are We Looking At?

Once we've found devices, we need to figure out what they are. Not all MIoT devices will neatly label themselves as "Life-Saving Ventilator Model X".

Key Fingerprinting Methods

MAC Address Lookup:

Every device has a vendor-assigned MAC prefix.

Use nmap --script mac-lookup or check sites like macvendors.com.

Example: A MAC prefix from GE Healthcare? Probably an MRI machine.

Service Enumeration:

Running nmap -sV will identify services like:

DICOM on Port 104 → Medical imaging system

HL7 on Port 2575 → Electronic Health Record (EHR) system

MQTT on Port 1883 → IoT telemetry device

Web-based UI on Port 443 → Could be an infusion pump, patient monitor, or even a pacemaker.

Banner Grabbing:

Some MIoT devices expose their firmware versions via HTTP headers or Telnet responses.

Run nc -v <IP> 80 or curl -I <IP> to see if the device tells you what it is.

📷 Pro Tip:

If you find a device with an outdated OpenSSH version, check Exploit-DB—there might be an RCE vulnerability just waiting to be exploited.

Step 4: Mapping & Organizing Device Data

Once we've identified all the devices, we need to document everything. Hospitals tend to lose track of equipment, so your work could save IT teams a world of pain later.

Best Practices for Device Inventory Management

✓ **Create a Master List**: Track device name, IP, MAC, services, vulnerabilities, and patch level.
✓ **Tag Critical Devices**: MRI scanners, infusion pumps, and PACS servers should be labeled high-risk.
✓ **Monitor for New Devices**: Use network monitoring tools to detect when new (or rogue) devices appear.

📷 Pro Tip:

Automate the process! Use Nmap scripts, SIEM tools, or Ansible playbooks to regularly update device inventories.

Final Thoughts: The Hunt Never Ends

Medical IoT devices are everywhere, but hospitals don't always know where all of them are. As security professionals, our first job is discovery. Whether you're a red teamer looking for attack surfaces or a blue teamer trying to secure the network, knowing what devices exist is half the battle.

So, put on your digital detective hat, scan responsibly, and remember: the more you know about the devices in your hospital, the less likely you'll be dealing with a ransomware crisis at 2 AM. 🎭

3.2 Using Shodan and Censys to Find Exposed Healthcare Systems

Alright, let's start with a question: What if I told you that you could find an unsecured MRI machine in a random hospital from the comfort of your couch—without hacking anything?

Sounds ridiculous, right? Welcome to the world of Shodan and Censys, where lazy administrators and misconfigured medical devices make for an IoT security goldmine.

Imagine a search engine like Google, but instead of finding cat videos, it finds unsecured hospital equipment, patient databases, and even entire ICU networks just chilling on the internet. That's Shodan and Censys in a nutshell. If you're a security researcher, penetration tester, or ethical hacker, these tools are like X-ray vision for the internet. And if you're a hospital administrator who just broke into a nervous sweat, don't worry—we'll also talk about how to defend against this insanity.

What Are Shodan and Censys?

Shodan: The "Search Engine for Hackers"

Unlike Google, which indexes web pages, Shodan indexes internet-connected devices. This includes everything from:

✓ MRI machines

✓ Infusion pumps

✓ PACS servers (medical imaging systems)

✓ Smart hospital beds

✓ Unsecured Electronic Health Record (EHR) databases

How does Shodan work?

It continuously scans the internet for open ports, services, and banners, then makes the results searchable.

Censys: Like Shodan, but Even More Aggressive

Censys operates similarly to Shodan but goes deeper into scanning TLS certificates, application-layer services, and even cloud misconfigurations.

If Shodan is like Google for IoT, Censys is like a hospital's worst nightmare in cybersecurity form.

Step 1: Hunting for Exposed Healthcare Systems with Shodan

Let's cut to the chase. If you want to find exposed medical IoT devices, you need the right search queries.

Basic Shodan Queries for Medical IoT

1️ Finding Exposed PACS (Medical Imaging) Servers

PACS servers store X-rays, MRIs, and CT scans. Many hospitals forget to secure them.

🔍 Shodan Query:

port:104 "DICOM"

Or

title:"DICOM server response"

👀 What you'll find:

Open PACS servers that anyone can access.

Patient images without authentication.

2️⃣ Finding Unsecured Electronic Health Records (EHR) Systems

EHRs store patient medical histories, prescriptions, and billing information.

🔍 Shodan Query:

title:"EMR" OR "EHR"

Or

port:443 "Electronic Medical Record"

👀 What you'll find:

Exposed login pages of hospital record systems.

Sometimes, default admin credentials still work (yikes).

3️⃣ Searching for Exposed Infusion Pumps and Smart Medical Devices

An infusion pump controls how much medication a patient receives. Hack one, and you can alter doses remotely.

🔍 Shodan Query:

port:23 "infusion"

Or

product:"Baxter" OR "Medtronic"

👀 What you'll find:

Internet-facing infusion pumps, possibly running Telnet (a major security fail).

4️⃣ Locating Unsecured Hospital Networks & VPNs

Many hospitals leave VPN gateways and remote access portals wide open.

🔍 Shodan Query:

"remote desktop" "hospital"

Or

port:3389 "Remote Desktop"

👀 What you'll find:

Exposed hospital administration systems.

Unprotected remote access points (a hacker's dream).

Step 2: Digging Deeper with Censys

Censys offers even more in-depth search capabilities, allowing you to query TLS certificates, IoT fingerprints, and misconfigured cloud services.

Basic Censys Queries for Medical IoT

1️⃣ Finding Medical IoT Devices by SSL Certificates

parsed.names: "hospital" AND services.service_name: "https"

👀 What you'll find:

Self-signed hospital SSL certs (often misconfigured).

Websites leaking internal hospital domains.

2️⃣ Finding Exposed Medical IoT Devices by Manufacturer

metadata.manufacturer: "GE Healthcare" OR "Siemens Healthineers"

👀 What you'll find:

MRI machines with remote access enabled.

Unpatched firmware versions (time for some CVE hunting).

Step 3: The Real-World Consequences of Exposed Medical Devices

Unfortunately, this isn't just theoretical. Hackers are already using Shodan and Censys to target hospitals.

📌 Case Study: Ransomware Attacks on Healthcare

WannaCry (2017): Shut down hospitals in the UK and US by exploiting unpatched Windows XP machines.

Ryuk Ransomware (2020): Used exposed RDP (Remote Desktop Protocol) servers to infect entire hospital networks.

📌 Case Study: MRI Machines Found on Shodan

In 2021, researchers found over 400 MRI machines directly exposed on the internet.

Many had default admin passwords like "admin/admin".

🔟 **Moral of the story**: If your hospital's devices are searchable on Shodan, they might as well be broadcasting their passwords on Twitter.

Step 4: Defending Against Shodan & Censys Exposure

Alright, so now that we've terrified everyone, how do we stop hospitals from becoming Shodan's next horror story?

🔒 How to Defend Against Exposure

✓ **Use a VPN**: Never expose MIoT devices directly to the internet.

✓ **Block Shodan Scanning**: Configure firewalls to deny known Shodan scanner IPs.

✓ **Patch and Update**: Many old hospital systems are vulnerable because they never get security updates.

✓ **Enforce Strong Authentication**: No more admin/password123 nonsense. Use 2FA and strong credentials.

✓ **Run Your Own Shodan Queries**: Regularly search for your own hospital's IP addresses and domains.

Final Thoughts: Hackers Don't Need to Break In—You're Inviting Them

Shodan and Censys aren't hacker tools—they're public information tools. The real problem is that hospitals and medical facilities keep exposing their critical systems.

If you're in healthcare IT, do yourself a favor:

Check Shodan for your own hospital's systems.

Patch your devices before ransomware gangs do it for you.

Stop leaving life-critical medical equipment open to the internet.

Because if a bored security researcher can find your MRI machine on Shodan, imagine what a ransomware gang can do. □

3.3 Passive and Active Network Scanning in Hospital Environments

Let's play a little game. Imagine you're a hacker (for ethical purposes, of course). You've just walked into a hospital lobby, grabbed a cup of bad coffee, and casually connected to the free guest Wi-Fi. Within minutes, you start seeing device names, IP addresses, and even unsecured medical equipment—all without touching a single keyboard command.

Congratulations! You've just performed passive network scanning—the art of eavesdropping on network traffic without actively probing anything. But let's not stop there. What if you wanted to go deeper? What if you could actively probe the hospital's network, find connected devices, and even identify misconfigured or vulnerable systems?

That's where active network scanning comes into play. But before we go full hacker mode, let's break down what passive vs. active scanning means, why hospitals are uniquely vulnerable, and how defenders can lock things down before attackers strike.

What Is Passive Network Scanning?

Passive network scanning is like listening in on a conversation without actually speaking. You don't send any packets, probe devices, or alert the network. Instead, you:

Monitor existing traffic (packets flying through the network).

Collect metadata from broadcasted signals (like Wi-Fi beacons).

Analyze open services and device behaviors without touching them.

Passive Scanning Techniques in Hospitals

✓ Listening to Broadcast Traffic

Many medical IoT devices shout their presence over the network.

You can catch device names, IPs, MAC addresses, and even login prompts.

✓ Sniffing Unencrypted Data

Many legacy hospital systems still transmit data in plaintext (yes, even patient records!).

Attackers can see usernames, passwords, and device data floating around.

✓ Detecting Unsecured Protocols

Telnet, FTP, and SNMPv1 are still shockingly common in hospitals.

Just listening for these protocols can tell an attacker where to strike.

Tools for Passive Scanning

🔍 **Wireshark** – The ultimate packet sniffer. Ideal for analyzing live network traffic.
🔍 **Kismet** – The go-to tool for wireless network sniffing.

🔍 **tcpdump** – A command-line packet capture tool. Lightweight but powerful.

📷 **Real-World Example:**

In 2022, security researchers found hundreds of exposed medical devices broadcasting sensitive patient data over unencrypted protocols—without hackers needing to do anything other than listen to network traffic.

What Is Active Network Scanning?

Now, let's talk about the louder (and riskier) cousin: active network scanning. Unlike passive scanning, this method sends requests to devices to see how they respond.

Imagine a doctor walking through a hospital tapping every door to see which ones are unlocked. That's what active scanning does—it actively probes devices to detect open ports, running services, and vulnerabilities.

Active Scanning Techniques in Hospitals

✔ Port Scanning

Finding open doors (ports) on hospital networks.

Common medical device ports: 104 (DICOM), 443 (HTTPS), 3389 (RDP), 9100 (Printers & PACS systems).

✔ Service Fingerprinting

Identifying which software versions are running.

Great for finding outdated and vulnerable systems.

✔ Vulnerability Scanning

Actively testing devices for security flaws.

Tools like Nmap, Nessus, and OpenVAS can reveal dangerous misconfigurations.

Tools for Active Scanning

🔍 **Nmap** – The king of network reconnaissance.
🔍 **Zmap** – A high-speed scanner for large networks.
🔍 **Nessus** – A powerful vulnerability scanner for finding weak spots.

💻 **Real-World Example:**

In 2021, a penetration test on a hospital network revealed over 1,000 devices with open RDP ports, allowing attackers to gain remote access to MRI machines and EHR systems.

Why Are Hospitals Uniquely Vulnerable?

1️⃣ Too Many Connected Devices

Hospitals are filled with medical IoT devices—and many are unpatched, old, or misconfigured.

2️⃣ Outdated Legacy Systems

Many hospitals still run Windows XP (yes, in 2025!), meaning they lack modern security protections.

3️⃣ Lack of Network Segmentation

If a hacker compromises one medical device, they often have access to the entire hospital network.

4️⃣ Compliance vs. Security Conflicts

Regulations like HIPAA focus on data privacy but don't always require strong cybersecurity measures.

Defending Against Network Scanning Attacks

Now that we've scared the hospital IT team, let's talk defense.

☐ How to Stop Passive Scanning

✓ **Use Encrypted Protocols (TLS, SSH, SFTP, etc.)** – No more plaintext traffic.

✓ **Limit Broadcast Traffic** – Medical devices shouldn't be shouting their existence.

✓ **Implement Network Monitoring** – If someone is sniffing way too much traffic, flag it.

☐ **How to Stop Active Scanning**

✓ **Segment Networks** – Keep medical IoT devices on separate VLANs.

✓ **Block Unnecessary Ports** – If port 23 (Telnet) is open, close it yesterday.

✓ **Use Intrusion Detection Systems (IDS)** – Detect and block scanning attempts in real-time.

◎ **Pro Tip:**

Want to see if your hospital's network is exposed?

Try running an Nmap scan on your internal devices (with permission, of course!) and see how many open ports and vulnerable services you find.

Final Thoughts: The Cybersecurity War Room

Hospitals are meant to heal people, not serve as playgrounds for hackers. Yet, every day, lazy configurations, old systems, and lack of security awareness make them prime targets.

Here's the hard truth:

If attackers can sniff your network, they can steal patient data.

If attackers can scan your devices, they can find a way in.

It's time for hospitals to fight back. That means securing networks, encrypting traffic, blocking unnecessary ports, and monitoring for suspicious activity.

Because if we don't start locking things down, hackers will keep walking in through the digital front door—and patients will pay the price.

3.4 Firmware and Software Fingerprinting for Vulnerability Analysis

Alright, picture this: You're a cybersecurity detective, and your latest case involves a mysterious, internet-connected MRI machine that's behaving… strangely. Maybe it's running slower than usual, or maybe it's suddenly communicating with a sketchy server in another country.

You suspect a security vulnerability, but where do you start?

Enter firmware and software fingerprinting—the cybersecurity equivalent of CSI for medical IoT devices. Just like a detective lifts fingerprints from a crime scene to identify a suspect, fingerprinting a device's firmware and software helps uncover vulnerabilities, outdated components, and hidden backdoors.

This chapter will walk you through:

What firmware and software fingerprinting is.

Why it's dangerous if attackers do it before you do.

How to fingerprint devices to find and fix vulnerabilities—before the bad guys exploit them.

Let's get hacking. (Ethically, of course.)

What Is Firmware and Software Fingerprinting?

Every medical IoT device—whether it's an insulin pump, a pacemaker, or a patient monitoring system—runs on firmware and software.

📌 Firmware vs. Software: What's the Difference?

✓ **Firmware** – The low-level code that controls hardware functionality (e.g., the code running on an MRI scanner's embedded chip).

✓ **Software** – The higher-level applications that interact with users and networks (e.g., the user interface of a hospital's imaging system).

Now, fingerprinting is the process of analyzing these components to determine:

What version the device is running.

Who developed it and whether it's been modified.

If it contains known vulnerabilities.

Think of it like checking a car's VIN number to see if it's been recalled for safety issues—except in this case, the "safety issue" could allow hackers to take control of a medical device.

Why Do Hackers Love Fingerprinting Medical IoT?

Because hospitals suck at updating devices.

Unlike your phone, which probably gets regular updates, many medical IoT devices haven't been patched in years—or can't be updated at all due to FDA restrictions and hospital bureaucracy.

● **What Attackers Can Learn from Fingerprinting**

Outdated firmware versions → If a device is running old firmware, attackers can search for known exploits.

Hardcoded credentials → Some firmware contains default admin passwords attackers can use.

Unpatched vulnerabilities → If the manufacturer hasn't issued a fix, the device is a sitting duck.

📷 **Real-World Example:**

In 2021, researchers discovered that certain hospital infusion pumps were running firmware from 2008—complete with hardcoded credentials and unencrypted communication protocols. A hacker with fingerprinting skills could easily exploit these weaknesses to remotely change medication dosages.

Fingerprinting Techniques for Vulnerability Analysis

Now that we know why fingerprinting matters, let's talk how to do it.

⬜⬜ Passive Fingerprinting (Stealth Mode)

Passive fingerprinting is like reading clues from a crime scene without touching anything. It involves analyzing network traffic to infer:

✓ **Device type** (Is it an MRI scanner? A patient monitor?)

✓ **Firmware version** (Is it outdated?)

✓ **Software signatures** (Are there known vulnerabilities?)

⬜ Tools for Passive Fingerprinting

🔍 **p0f** – Identifies devices and OS versions from network traffic.
🔍 **Wireshark** – Sniffs packets to detect device behavior and software versions.
🔍 **Shodan** – Finds internet-connected medical devices exposed to the web.

🔊 **Pro Tip**: If a medical device is broadcasting old firmware version numbers, an attacker doesn't even have to hack it—they just Google the version number + "exploit" and see what pops up.

🔍 Active Fingerprinting (Red Team Mode)

Active fingerprinting is more aggressive. It involves interacting with the device to pull firmware/software details directly.

Common techniques include:

✓ **Port Scanning** – Checking which services and protocols are open.

✓ **Banner Grabbing** – Extracting device metadata from error messages and login prompts.

✓ **Firmware Extraction** – Pulling firmware directly from a device to analyze its contents.

⬜ Tools for Active Fingerprinting

🔍 **Nmap** – Can detect OS versions, services, and even firmware details.
🔍 **Binwalk** – Extracts firmware from medical devices for reverse engineering.
🔍 **JTAGulator** – A tool to connect to hardware debugging interfaces.

📷 **Real-World Example:**

A security researcher extracted firmware from a hospital ultrasound machine and found an old SSH private key that allowed remote access to thousands of devices worldwide. Yikes.

Protecting Medical IoT Devices from Fingerprinting Attacks

Alright, we've covered how fingerprinting works, now let's talk how to stop attackers from using it against hospitals.

☐☐ 1. Keep Firmware and Software Updated

If the manufacturer releases a security patch, install it.

Push vendors for regular updates (or replace outdated devices!).

☐☐ 2. Obfuscate Device Information

Configure devices to hide firmware version numbers from login banners.

Use TLS encryption so passive sniffers can't read unencrypted traffic.

☐☐ 3. Segment Networks

Don't let MRI machines and patient monitors sit on the same network as guest Wi-Fi.

Isolate critical devices to minimize attack surfaces.

☐☐ 4. Monitor for Unauthorized Scans

Use Intrusion Detection Systems (IDS) to detect fingerprinting attempts.

Block or alert on suspicious Nmap or Shodan-style scans.

🚨 **Final Warning**: If you're in a hospital's IT security team, try fingerprinting your own devices before the hackers do. You'll be shocked at what you find.

Final Thoughts: Fingerprinting Is Inevitable—So Stay Ahead of Hackers

At the end of the day, fingerprinting is a double-edged sword.

Hackers use it to find and exploit vulnerabilities in medical IoT devices.

Security professionals use it to detect and fix those vulnerabilities first.

The real danger? Many hospitals aren't doing either—leaving their networks wide open for attackers to fingerprint, exploit, and compromise critical healthcare systems.

So here's the challenge: Start fingerprinting your own devices today. Learn what an attacker would see, and start fixing those security gaps before they turn into headlines about another hospital breach.

Because in cybersecurity, knowing is half the battle—and acting before the bad guys do is the other half.

3.5 Defensive Strategies for Reducing Exposure

Alright, let's play a game. You're a hacker, and your mission is to break into a hospital's network and mess with its medical IoT devices. You fire up Shodan, scan for vulnerable infusion pumps, and—bam!—you find one running firmware from 2012. Jackpot.

But just as you're about to launch your exploit, something strange happens. The device isn't responding the way you expected. Your IP gets blocked. The network is segmented. Your attack fails.

That, my friends, is what a well-defended Medical IoT ecosystem looks like.

In this chapter, we're flipping the script—you're no longer the hacker; you're the defender. Your job is to make sure hospitals, medical devices, and patient data stay out of the wrong hands. Let's talk about how to reduce attack exposure before bad actors even get a chance to strike.

Why Reducing Attack Exposure Matters in Medical IoT

Medical IoT devices are sitting ducks for cyberattacks. Unlike corporate laptops that get patched regularly, many MRI machines, patient monitors, and infusion pumps run ancient, unpatched firmware.

Here's why that's terrifying:

✓ Medical IoT devices control life-critical functions.

✓ Most hospitals don't even know all the devices on their network.

✓ Attackers are already scanning for weak points—constantly.

Reducing exposure means:

Making devices harder to find (so attackers can't fingerprint them).

Implementing security layers (so even if one layer fails, others hold strong).

Proactively fixing vulnerabilities (before an exploit takes down an entire hospital).

Step 1: Know What You Have (Asset Inventory & Visibility)

You can't defend what you don't even know exists.

One of the biggest problems in hospitals is shadow IoT—devices that were deployed without IT's knowledge. A rogue doctor plugs in a smart medical device for convenience, and suddenly, there's an unprotected endpoint connected to patient records.

🔥 **Defensive Strategy: Conduct a Full Asset Inventory**

✓ **Use Active and Passive Scanning** – Run network scans to find all medical IoT devices (but do it carefully to avoid disrupting patient care).

✓ **Map Every Device to a Security Policy** – Every IoT device should have clear access control rules.

✓ **Monitor Network Behavior Continuously** – Deploy Intrusion Detection Systems (IDS) to detect new or suspicious devices.

Pro Tip: Tools like Armis, Medigate, and Cynerio specialize in healthcare device security monitoring.

Step 2: Hide Your Devices (Network Segmentation & Access Controls)

If an attacker can't see your device, they can't hack it.

Most hospitals still have flat networks, meaning medical IoT devices share the same network as patient databases, workstations, and even guest Wi-Fi.

This is a disaster waiting to happen.

🔥 **Defensive Strategy: Implement Network Segmentation**

✓ **Medical IoT VLANs** – Keep life-critical devices separate from general IT systems.

✓ **Zero Trust Architecture** – No device should be trusted by default, even if it's inside the hospital network.

✓ **MAC Address Whitelisting** – Only pre-approved devices should be able to connect to medical networks.

Real-World Example: When the WannaCry ransomware attack hit hospitals worldwide in 2017, many affected networks had poor segmentation, allowing the malware to spread rapidly.

Step 3: Lock Down Remote Access & Cloud Connectivity

With the rise of telemedicine and remote patient monitoring, medical IoT devices are more internet-connected than ever. This is both a convenience and a nightmare.

✓ Attackers love exposed IoT devices because they can remotely exploit them without stepping foot in a hospital.

✓ Weak API security in telehealth platforms can leak patient data or allow remote device manipulation.

🔥 **Defensive Strategy: Secure Remote Access**

✓ **Disable Unnecessary Remote Access** – If a device doesn't need internet access, cut it off.

✓ **Enforce Strong API Authentication** – Use OAuth2, JWT, and rate-limiting to prevent abuse.

✓ **Monitor Outbound Traffic** – Medical IoT devices should NOT be talking to random servers in foreign countries.

🔊 **Fun Fact**: Some hospital devices still use Telnet for remote access. If you see this, grab a fire extinguisher because your network is already on fire.

Step 4: Harden Medical IoT Firmware and Software

Many medical IoT vulnerabilities come from weak firmware security—outdated code, hardcoded credentials, and unpatched exploits.

✓ Some devices still ship with default admin passwords like admin/admin.

✓ Attackers can extract firmware from a medical device and analyze it for backdoors and exploits.

🔥 **Defensive Strategy: Secure Firmware & Software**

✓ **Enforce Regular Updates** – Work with vendors to push security patches (even if they resist).

✓ **Remove Default Credentials** – Change hardcoded passwords before deploying a device.

✓ **Enable Secure Boot** – Prevent unauthorized firmware modifications.

🔊 **Scary Reality**: A study found that 75% of medical IoT devices run outdated operating systems with known security flaws. If that doesn't scare you, I don't know what will.

Step 5: Monitor, Detect, and Respond in Real-Time

Even with all the defenses above, assume attackers will still try to get in. Your job is to catch them early—before they cause real damage.

◖ Defensive Strategy: Real-Time Threat Detection

✓ **Deploy Medical IoT Security Platforms** – Tools like Armis, Medigate, or CyberMDX can detect abnormal device behavior.

✓ **Use SIEM for Log Analysis** – Feed medical IoT logs into a Security Information and Event Management (SIEM) system.

✓ **Set Up Automated Response Mechanisms** – If an MRI machine suddenly starts sending data to China, block it immediately.

🖥 **Red Team Tip**: Simulate attacks on your own hospital network. If you can break into it, so can a real hacker. Fix the gaps before they do.

Final Thoughts: You Can't Stop All Attacks, But You Can Reduce Exposure

Here's the deal:

✓ Hackers are scanning for medical IoT vulnerabilities right now.

✓ Hospitals can't afford to wait until AFTER an attack happens.

✓ Reducing exposure means making devices harder to find, exploit, and manipulate.

If you work in healthcare IT or cybersecurity, you're on the frontlines of digital patient safety.

Your job isn't just protecting networks—it's protecting lives.

So go forth, harden those devices, segment those networks, and make life miserable for hackers. Because if an attacker comes for your hospital and finds nothing but dead ends and blocked access, you've already won.

Chapter 4: Attacking Medical IoT Networks

You ever hear about a hacker getting into a hospital network just by plugging a Raspberry Pi into an exposed Ethernet port? Yeah, that happens. If you think hospital networks are locked down like Fort Knox, think again. Weak configurations, outdated firewall rules, and unsecured APIs make medical networks a playground for cybercriminals. And once they're inside? Let's just say your medical records might end up on the dark web before your doctor even gets a chance to read them.

This chapter explores common attacks on medical IoT networks, including man-in-the-middle (MITM) exploits, SSL stripping, ARP poisoning, and firewall evasion techniques. We'll discuss how attackers bypass traditional security measures and how defenders can implement network hardening strategies to mitigate these threats. Given the critical nature of healthcare environments, securing network infrastructure is essential to prevent unauthorized access, data breaches, and potential patient harm.

4.1 Exploiting Weak Network Configurations in Hospitals

Picture this: You walk into a hospital, coffee in one hand, laptop in the other. You casually connect to the "Guest Wi-Fi", open a few browser tabs, and—out of curiosity—you fire up a network scanner. Within seconds, you see unsecured medical devices, unencrypted traffic, and an admin panel with no login credentials.

Congratulations! You've just hacked a hospital's network—without even trying.

Now, if this were a Hollywood movie, alarms would go off, security guards would rush in, and you'd have to escape through the air vents. But in reality? No one even notices. That's the terrifying truth about weak hospital network security—it's easy to exploit, often ignored, and incredibly dangerous.

Welcome to the dark side of medical IoT security, where a poorly configured network can mean life-or-death consequences. Let's break down how attackers exploit weak hospital networks—and, more importantly, how to stop them.

Why Hospital Networks Are a Hacker's Playground

Hospitals aren't like corporate offices. They have a messy mix of old and new technology, and security is often an afterthought. Here's why most hospital networks are ridiculously easy to exploit:

✓ **Flat Networks** – Many hospitals have zero network segmentation, meaning MRI machines, infusion pumps, and patient records all sit on the same network as guest Wi-Fi and cafeteria POS systems.

✓ **Legacy Devices** – Some medical devices still run Windows XP (yes, seriously) and can't be patched.

✓ **Default Credentials** – Too many admin panels, routers, and IoT devices still use default logins like admin/password.

✓ **Unsecured APIs & Cloud Services** – Patient data is transmitted unencrypted or stored in misconfigured cloud databases.

For an attacker, this is heaven. They don't even need elite hacking skills—just basic network scanning and exploitation techniques.

Step 1: Mapping the Network (Because Hospitals Don't Even Know What's Connected)

Before exploiting a network, an attacker needs to understand its structure. In hospitals, this is shockingly easy because most IT teams don't even have a full inventory of their devices.

✓ **Shodan & Censys** – Attackers can scan for exposed hospital devices from the comfort of their couch.

✓ **Nmap & Angry IP Scanner** – A quick scan inside the hospital network can reveal every connected device, open port, and service running.

✓ **Wireshark** – Sniffing network traffic often reveals unencrypted patient data and login credentials flying through the air.

🔎 **Real-World Example**: Researchers found a hospital's drug infusion pump accessible over the internet—with no authentication required. Attackers could have remotely altered medication dosages without anyone noticing.

Step 2: Exploiting Weak Network Segmentation

Scenario: Imagine you walk into a hospital, connect to the public Wi-Fi, and within minutes, you're inside the internal network that controls MRI machines, ventilators, and patient databases.

Sounds impossible? It happens all the time.

✓ Most hospitals don't segment their networks properly.

✓ Medical devices are often connected to the same network as staff computers.

✓ Once an attacker gets inside, they can move laterally with ease.

🔥 **How Attackers Exploit This:**

Pivoting Attacks – Once inside the network, attackers use tools like ProxyChains or Metasploit to jump from one device to another.

MITM (Man-in-the-Middle) Attacks – Since devices are poorly isolated, attackers can intercept traffic, steal credentials, and alter medical data.

Ransomware Deployment – If malware infects one vulnerable system, it can spread hospital-wide in minutes.

📖 **Case Study: WannaCry Ransomware (2017)** – UK hospitals were crippled because their networks were flat—allowing the ransomware to spread across entire hospital systems instantly.

Step 3: Attacking Unsecured Medical APIs & Cloud Services

With the rise of telemedicine and remote healthcare, hospitals now rely on APIs and cloud services to store and share patient data. But here's the problem:

✓ APIs are often exposed without authentication.

✓ Cloud databases are misconfigured and left open to the public.

✓ Patient data is transmitted in plaintext (no encryption).

🔥 **How Attackers Exploit This:**

Brute Force Attacks on APIs – Many APIs still allow unlimited login attempts, making them easy targets for credential stuffing.

Cloud Misconfigurations – Attackers can scan for open AWS S3 buckets and steal sensitive medical records.

SQL Injection & API Abuse – Poorly secured EHR (Electronic Health Record) systems often have SQL injection vulnerabilities that let hackers extract entire patient databases.

🏮 **Scary Reality**: A 2022 report found that 30% of healthcare cloud storage services had exposed patient data—without even needing a password.

Step 4: Exploiting Weak Hospital Wi-Fi Security

Let's talk about hospital Wi-Fi—because honestly, it's a joke.

✓ Many hospitals still use WEP encryption (which can be cracked in minutes).

✓ Some Wi-Fi networks share the same credentials for months or years.

✓ IoT devices connect via Wi-Fi with weak authentication.

🔥 **How Attackers Exploit This:**

Deauth Attacks – Attackers can use aircrack-ng to force disconnect devices, then capture their handshake and crack the Wi-Fi password.

Evil Twin Attacks – A hacker sets up a fake hospital Wi-Fi and waits for staff to connect and enter their credentials.

Intercepting Medical Device Traffic – Many wireless infusion pumps, patient monitors, and wearable health devices don't encrypt their data—making them easy to manipulate.

🏮 **Red Team Insight**: I've personally seen hospitals where the same Wi-Fi password was used for five years straight. An attacker could literally sit in the parking lot and access the hospital's internal systems without stepping inside.

Defensive Strategies: How to Lock Down Hospital Networks

So how do we stop all this madness? Here's how hospitals should defend themselves (but often don't):

✓ **Network Segmentation** – Medical IoT devices should be on isolated VLANs, completely separate from staff and public networks.

✓ **Disable Unnecessary Open Ports** – Block everything that isn't needed for critical operations.

✓ **Enforce Strong API Authentication** – Use OAuth2, rate-limiting, and encrypted API keys.

✓ **Regularly Rotate Wi-Fi Credentials** – And ban WEP/WPA1 encryption forever.

✓ **Deploy IDS/IPS Systems** – Use network monitoring tools to detect unauthorized access in real-time.

✓ **Update and Patch Devices** – If a device can't be patched, replace it or isolate it.

🚨 **Final Warning**: If hospitals don't start fixing these basic security flaws, hackers will continue exploiting them with ease. It's not a question of if—but when.

Final Thoughts: Hospitals Need to Get Their Act Together

Hackers don't need to be geniuses to break into hospital networks. They just need patience and a Wi-Fi adapter.

If a hospital's network is poorly configured, an attacker can:

✓ Steal patient data

✓ Take over life-critical devices

✓ Shut down hospital operations with ransomware

So, hospitals—secure your damn networks. Your patients' lives literally depend on it.

4.2 MITM Attacks on Medical IoT Devices (SSL Stripping, ARP Poisoning)

Alright, let's talk about Man-in-the-Middle (MITM) attacks—the cybercriminal equivalent of eavesdropping on a private conversation while casually sipping coffee nearby. Except, instead of overhearing someone's awkward breakup at a café, an attacker is quietly intercepting and manipulating data flowing between medical IoT devices, hospital systems, and patients.

Imagine you're wearing a smart heart monitor that transmits real-time ECG data to your doctor. Now, picture a hacker silently slipping between that connection, reading, altering, or even injecting false data into the system. One minute your heart rate looks fine, the next—boom—it shows a critical emergency, and an ambulance is sent racing to your house for no reason.

Scary, right?

MITM attacks are dangerously common in medical IoT, yet hospitals and device manufacturers often fail to implement even basic defenses. Let's dive into how MITM attacks work, how they're used against medical IoT devices, and how to stop them before someone turns your pacemaker into a DJ turntable.

How MITM Attacks Work in Medical IoT

MITM attacks occur when an attacker intercepts communication between two devices without either party realizing it. They can do this by:

Interception: The hacker positions themselves between the victim's device and the network.

Data Manipulation: They can steal sensitive data (like medical records or credentials) or modify transmitted information (e.g., changing dosage instructions in an insulin pump).

Session Hijacking: They take control of an active session, impersonating a trusted device or user.

For medical IoT, MITM attacks target unsecured wireless transmissions, hospital networks, and poorly protected APIs. Two of the most dangerous techniques used in these attacks are SSL Stripping and ARP Poisoning.

SSL Stripping: Downgrading Secure Connections to Steal Data

Let's say you're visiting a hospital's patient portal. You expect your browser to use HTTPS (encrypted communication). But what if I told you that an attacker could downgrade your connection to HTTP, making it completely unencrypted? That's exactly what SSL Stripping does.

◆ How SSL Stripping Works:

The victim (you) tries to connect to a secure website (e.g., https://hospitalrecords.com).

The attacker intercepts the request and forwards it to the server using HTTP instead of HTTPS.

The server responds, but the victim's browser is unknowingly communicating over an unencrypted connection.

The attacker reads and modifies all traffic in real-time, stealing patient data, credentials, and session tokens.

🏛 **Real-World Example**: In 2019, researchers found that many hospital portals failed to enforce HTTPS, allowing MITM attackers to capture login credentials and steal patient medical records.

🔥 Why SSL Stripping Works in Medical IoT:

Many legacy medical devices don't support HTTPS, making them easy targets.

Poorly configured hospital networks don't enforce encryption between IoT devices and cloud services.

Some medical APIs still accept HTTP requests, leaving data wide open for attackers.

ARP Poisoning: Hijacking Network Traffic in Hospitals

Address Resolution Protocol (ARP) Poisoning is an old-school hacking trick that still works shockingly well in modern hospitals.

◆ How ARP Poisoning Works:

Every device on a network uses ARP to map IP addresses to MAC addresses (like a digital phonebook).

An attacker tricks devices into thinking their MAC address belongs to the hospital's gateway router.

All traffic from medical devices and hospital computers now flows through the attacker before reaching its destination.

The attacker can steal login credentials, read patient data, modify drug dosages, or inject malware into medical IoT devices.

🏛 **Hospital Horror Story**: In a penetration test, security researchers used ARP poisoning to intercept doctors' login credentials at a hospital. Within minutes, they gained access to electronic health records (EHRs), medical imaging systems, and even remote surgery tools.

🔥 **Why ARP Poisoning Works in Medical IoT:**

Hospital networks are often poorly segmented, allowing attackers to target medical IoT devices from any compromised system.

Many medical IoT devices don't use strong authentication, making them easy to impersonate.

Encryption is not enforced at the network level, so data can be captured in plaintext.

MITM Attack Scenarios in Smart Healthcare

To see how devastating MITM attacks can be, let's look at some realistic attack scenarios in medical IoT:

Scenario 1: Hijacking a Smart Infusion Pump

An attacker inside a hospital uses ARP poisoning to intercept traffic between a nurse's workstation and an IoT-controlled infusion pump. The attacker:

✓ Reads real-time dosage instructions.

✓ Modifies the drug dosage remotely, increasing or decreasing medication levels.

✓ Locks the infusion pump, demanding a ransom to restore functionality.

☞ **Consequence**: The patient receives a lethal overdose or no medication at all.

Scenario 2: Fake Test Results in a Telemedicine System

A cybercriminal launches an SSL Stripping attack on a remote patient monitoring system. They:

✓ Intercept and modify ECG data sent from a patient's wearable heart monitor.

✓ Replace normal heart rate readings with dangerously high values.

✓ Cause doctors to prescribe unnecessary treatments—or even hospitalize the patient.

☞ **Consequence**: False medical emergencies, incorrect treatments, and unnecessary surgeries.

Defensive Strategies: How to Stop MITM Attacks in Healthcare

Hospitals and medical IoT manufacturers need to step up their security game. Here's how they can prevent MITM attacks:

✓ **Enforce HTTPS Everywhere** – Use HSTS (HTTP Strict Transport Security) to force encrypted connections on all medical websites and APIs.

✓ **Implement Network Segmentation** – Separate medical IoT devices, hospital workstations, and guest networks to limit lateral movement.

✓ **Use ARP Spoofing Detection Tools** – Deploy Intrusion Detection Systems (IDS) to monitor for suspicious ARP activity.

✓ **Encrypt All Internal Traffic** – Use TLS encryption for data transmitted between medical devices and hospital systems.

✓ **Deploy DNSSEC & VPNs** – Protect internal communications with secure DNS protocols and end-to-end encryption.

✓ **Regular Security Audits** – Test medical IoT systems for vulnerabilities in encryption, authentication, and network security.

🔊 **Final Warning**: If hospitals don't take these attacks seriously, it's only a matter of time before hackers start manipulating medical data on a massive scale.

Final Thoughts: Your Pacemaker Shouldn't Be Hackable

MITM attacks in medical IoT aren't just theoretical risks—they're happening right now, and most hospitals have no idea.

If an attacker can intercept and manipulate life-critical data from a pacemaker, insulin pump, or ventilator, they have the power to kill patients remotely. That's not paranoia—that's reality.

So, to all hospitals and medical device manufacturers out there:

Fix. Your. Security.

Or don't—just don't be surprised when your "smart" medical devices start sending doctors on wild goose chases and causing medical chaos.

4.3 Bypassing Firewalls and Intrusion Detection in Medical Environments

Alright, let's be honest—firewalls and intrusion detection systems (IDS) are like hospital security guards. They're meant to keep the bad guys out, but if you know the right tricks, you can stroll right past them with nothing more than a clipboard and a confident nod.

Now, in a hospital setting, we're not talking about sneaking into the cafeteria for an extra slice of cake (though I fully support that mission). We're talking about penetrating medical networks, slipping past firewalls, and avoiding intrusion detection to access electronic health records (EHRs), connected medical devices, and other critical infrastructure.

Unfortunately, many healthcare networks are still running outdated firewall rules, misconfigured IDS solutions, or—worse—no IDS at all. This makes them prime targets for attackers looking to bypass security controls and infiltrate sensitive systems.

So, how do hackers bypass firewalls and intrusion detection in medical environments? Let's dive into their favorite tactics, the weaknesses in current security measures, and most importantly—how to stop them before your hospital network turns into a hacker's playground.

Understanding the Role of Firewalls and IDS in Healthcare

Before we talk about breaking in, let's first understand what we're breaking past.

Firewalls: The First Line of Defense (Or Not?)

A firewall is essentially a digital gatekeeper that filters incoming and outgoing traffic based on a set of rules. In hospitals, firewalls are supposed to:

✓ Block unauthorized access to medical IoT devices, EHRs, and critical systems.

✓ Prevent malicious traffic from entering the network.

✓ Restrict access between different hospital departments and IoT zones.

However, many medical firewalls are configured poorly (or worse, outdated), making them a false sense of security rather than an actual barrier.

Intrusion Detection Systems (IDS): The Watchdogs

An IDS is designed to detect suspicious activity and alert administrators when something shady is happening. It can be:

Signature-Based IDS: Detects known attack patterns (like recognizing a famous hacker's "greatest hits" playlist).

Anomaly-Based IDS: Flags unusual behavior (like a nurse's workstation suddenly trying to access 1,000 patient records at once).

But here's the problem—many hospital IDS setups suffer from poor tuning, excessive false alarms, or lack of active monitoring. If an alert goes off and no one is there to see it, does it even matter?

How Hackers Bypass Firewalls in Medical Networks

Now that we know what these security tools do, let's talk about how attackers sidestep them like a doctor avoiding paperwork.

1. Using Tunneling and Encapsulation to Sneak Through Firewalls

Most hospital firewalls are configured to block unauthorized access but allow essential services (like DNS, HTTP, and HTTPS traffic) to pass freely. Attackers abuse this loophole by:

✓ **DNS Tunneling** – Hiding malicious traffic inside normal-looking DNS queries to bypass firewall restrictions.

✓ **ICMP Tunneling** – Using ping requests as a covert channel to exfiltrate patient data.

✓ **SSH and VPN Over Port 443** – Disguising malicious traffic as regular HTTPS connections.

☞ **Example**: A hacker sets up a reverse shell over a DNS tunnel to exfiltrate patient records without triggering firewall rules.

2. Exploiting Poorly Configured Firewall Rules

Many hospital firewalls suffer from terrible configuration mistakes, such as:

Overly permissive rules (e.g., "Allow all outbound traffic" □♂□).

Legacy systems with hardcoded exceptions (e.g., "Let this 10-year-old MRI machine talk to everything").

No segmentation between medical devices and general hospital networks.

☞ **Example**: A hacker compromises an IoT blood pressure monitor, then uses it to pivot deeper into the hospital network because the firewall treats all internal traffic as trusted.

3. Leveraging Application-Layer Attacks

Firewalls generally focus on network-layer filtering, but attackers target the application layer to bypass them. Some favorite tricks include:

✓ **SQL Injection & API Exploits** – Attacking vulnerable EHR portals and telemedicine APIs to extract sensitive data.

✓ **Cross-Site Scripting (XSS) & CSRF** – Injecting malicious scripts to steal credentials and session tokens.

✓ **Man-in-the-Middle (MITM) Attacks** – Intercepting medical traffic before it even reaches the firewall.

☞ **Example**: A hacker injects malicious SQL queries into a hospital's online patient portal, pulling entire patient databases—all while the firewall happily allows the request.

How Attackers Evade Intrusion Detection Systems (IDS) in Hospitals

Firewalls are one thing, but what about IDS? How do hackers slip past detection and remain unnoticed?

1. Blending in With Normal Traffic

Hospitals generate massive amounts of legitimate network traffic, and attackers take advantage of this to hide in plain sight.

✓ **Slow and Low Attacks** – Instead of launching a brute-force attack in seconds, attackers spread it out over days or weeks to stay under IDS thresholds.

✓ **Encrypting Malicious Traffic** – Many IDS setups don't inspect encrypted HTTPS traffic, allowing attackers to communicate freely inside an SSL tunnel.

✓ **Masquerading as a Legitimate User** – Using stolen doctor credentials to move around undetected.

☞ **Example**: Instead of hammering an EHR system with login attempts, an attacker tries one password per hour—slow enough to avoid triggering an IDS alert.

2. Modifying Attack Signatures to Avoid Detection

Signature-based IDS relies on known attack patterns, but hackers evolve their methods to avoid detection.

✓ **Polymorphic Malware** – Modifies its code each time it executes to prevent signature matching.

✓ **Encoding Payloads** – Using Base64, XOR, or obfuscation to hide attack commands.

✓ **Custom Payloads** – Slightly altering attack code to bypass known IDS signatures.

☞ **Example**: A hacker modifies a buffer overflow attack's payload by adding harmless code snippets, fooling the IDS into thinking it's normal traffic.

Defensive Strategies: Stopping Firewall and IDS Evasion

Hospitals need to wake up and stop treating firewalls and IDS like a magical security cure-all. Here's how to actually secure medical networks:

✔ **Implement Network Segmentation** – Separate medical devices, EHR systems, and general hospital networks to contain breaches.

✔ **Deep Packet Inspection (DPI)** – Monitor encrypted traffic to detect hidden threats.

✔ **Strict Firewall Rules** – Block unnecessary outbound connections and limit IoT devices to only essential communications.

✔ **Harden API Security** – Use authentication, rate limiting, and encryption to prevent application-layer attacks.

✔ **Deploy AI-Based Anomaly Detection** – Use machine learning IDS solutions to detect unusual patterns in real-time.

Final Thoughts: Hackers Love Lazy Defenses

Here's the deal—if your firewalls are misconfigured and your IDS is just collecting dust, you're already owned.

Hackers thrive on weak security policies, outdated defenses, and poor monitoring. The easier it is to bypass firewalls and IDS, the faster an attacker can exfiltrate medical data or manipulate IoT devices.

So, dear hospitals: Fix your security before someone turns your MRI machine into a crypto-mining rig.

4.4 Attacking Unsecured APIs in Telemedicine and EHR Systems

Alright, let's talk about APIs—the unsung heroes of the telemedicine and Electronic Health Record (EHR) revolution. These little gateways are what allow doctors to pull up patient records, send prescriptions, and schedule virtual consultations at the click of a button. Sounds convenient, right?

Well, they're also a hacker's dream.

You see, many medical APIs are about as secure as a diary with a broken lock. Misconfigurations, weak authentication, and lazy coding turn these APIs into the perfect entry point for attackers looking to steal patient data, manipulate prescriptions, or even remotely control connected medical devices.

Let's break down how hackers exploit unsecured APIs in healthcare, why telemedicine is a goldmine for cybercriminals, and—most importantly—how to lock things down before your EHR system becomes the next cybercrime headline.

Understanding Medical APIs: The Backbone of Connected Healthcare

Before we start breaking things, let's understand what we're dealing with.

What is an API in Healthcare?

An Application Programming Interface (API) is basically a middleman that allows different systems to communicate. In healthcare, APIs are used for things like:

✓ **Telemedicine platforms** (connecting patients and doctors)

✓ **EHR access** (retrieving patient medical records)

✓ **Medical IoT device control** (like insulin pumps and heart monitors)

✓ **Prescription management systems** (e-prescriptions and pharmacy updates)

For example, when a doctor logs into a telemedicine platform and retrieves a patient's records, the system isn't just magically displaying data. Instead, it's calling an API endpoint like:

GET /patient/records?patientID=12345

And if that API isn't secured properly? A hacker could make the same request, replacing "12345" with someone else's ID, and BOOM—instant data breach.

Why Are Medical APIs a Huge Target?

✓ They contain sensitive patient data (PHI is worth $$$ on the dark web).

✓ Many are exposed to the internet with weak security.

✓ They are often misconfigured—allowing unauthorized access.

✓ Telemedicine adoption has skyrocketed, but security hasn't caught up.

Now, let's get into the juicy part—how hackers exploit these weak APIs.

Common API Attacks in Telemedicine and EHR Systems

1. Broken Authentication: Who Needs a Password Anyway?

Imagine a hospital API that allows doctors to view patient records—but forgets to properly verify user identity. If authentication is weak, an attacker can:

✓ Log in using default or leaked credentials.

✓ Exploit weak password policies (like "admin123" □♂□).

✓ Bypass authentication entirely (if the API allows open access).

☞ **Example Attack:**

A hacker finds an API that allows:

GET /patient/records?patientID=12345

If there's no authentication check, they can just change the ID:

GET /patient/records?patientID=12346

…and start downloading everyone's medical history.

🔒 **Fix It**: Always use strong authentication mechanisms (OAuth, API keys, JWT tokens) and never expose sensitive endpoints without proper access control.

2. Unencrypted API Traffic: Sniffing Medical Data Like a Pro

Some hospitals still use unencrypted HTTP APIs instead of secure HTTPS. This means that if an attacker sniffs network traffic, they can steal API requests in plain text.

☞ **Example Attack:**

An attacker connects to a hospital's Wi-Fi and captures:

POST /api/login
username=drsmith&password=password123

Congratulations! The hacker now has Dr. Smith's credentials—and full access to patient records.

🔒 **Fix It**: Always encrypt API communications using TLS 1.2 or higher. Unencrypted medical data should be illegal at this point.

3. Insecure Direct Object References (IDOR): The Easiest Data Theft Ever

IDOR happens when an API allows unauthorized access to data, just by tweaking a request.

☞ **Example Attack:**

A telemedicine API call:

GET /appointment/details?userID=5678

What if an attacker changes the userID?

GET /appointment/details?userID=5679

If there's no proper access control, they've just stolen another patient's medical data.

🔒 **Fix It:** Always implement access control checks on API endpoints. Just because a request is valid doesn't mean it should be allowed.

4. Exploiting Weak API Endpoints for Remote Code Execution (RCE)

Some medical APIs allow doctors to send commands to IoT devices, like insulin pumps or pacemakers. If an attacker finds an insecure endpoint, they might be able to:

✓ Inject malicious commands into the API.

✓ Remotely control or disable medical devices.

✓ Execute arbitrary code on hospital servers.

☞ **Example Attack:**

A poorly secured API lets doctors update medical device firmware using:

POST /device/updateFirmware?deviceID=9876&file=update.bin

An attacker uploads a malicious firmware file, granting backdoor access to the device.

🔒 **Fix It**: Always validate and sanitize API inputs, and use strong authentication for API calls.

5. Lack of Rate Limiting: When Bots Steal All the Data

Many APIs don't limit the number of requests a user can make. This means attackers can scrape thousands of patient records in minutes using automation.

☞ **Example Attack:**

A hacker runs a simple script:

for i in range(10000):
*   requests.get(f"https://hospital.com/api/patient?ID={i}")*

Within seconds, they've downloaded an entire hospital's patient database.

🔒 **Fix It**: Use rate limiting (e.g., 5 requests per minute per user) and IP blocking to stop brute-force data theft.

Defensive Strategies: How to Secure Medical APIs

✓ **Use Strong Authentication**: Require OAuth, API keys, JWT tokens, and multi-factor authentication (MFA).

✓ **Encrypt API Traffic**: No unencrypted HTTP APIs—TLS 1.2 or higher only.

✓ **Validate User Permissions**: Ensure users can only access their own data.

✓ **Implement Rate Limiting**: Prevent brute-force attacks and data scraping.

✓ **Sanitize Inputs & Use Web Application Firewalls (WAFs):** Block SQL injection, XSS, and malicious API requests.

✓ **Monitor API Logs**: Detect suspicious API activity before it becomes a full-blown breach.

Final Thoughts: Hackers Love Lazy API Security

If your hospital's API security is as loose as a broken IV line, you're asking for trouble.

Hackers know that healthcare organizations are slow to patch vulnerabilities, and they love APIs that expose sensitive data with little to no security. If you're running a telemedicine platform or an EHR system, it's time to lock things down before someone exploits your system—or worse, manipulates medical devices remotely.

So, dear hospital IT teams: Secure your APIs before your patient data ends up in a hacker's personal health record.

4.5 Hardening Network Security in Healthcare Environments

Let's be honest—healthcare networks are like overworked doctors: too busy, underfunded, and one bad day away from a total breakdown. Between legacy systems, unsecured IoT devices, and staff who still use "password123" (looking at you, Dr. Smith), hospitals are prime targets for cyberattacks.

Hackers love healthcare environments because they're full of sensitive patient data, life-saving devices, and weak security. Ransomware gangs, nation-state attackers, and cybercriminals know that hospitals can't afford downtime, making them high-value, low-effort targets.

So, how do we lock things down and turn a soft, easy-to-hack healthcare network into a digital fortress? Let's break it down.

Understanding the Healthcare Attack Surface

Before we start hardening security, let's talk about what needs protection.

A modern healthcare environment includes:

✓ **Electronic Health Record (EHR) systems** – Store sensitive patient data.

✓ **Medical IoT devices** – Infusion pumps, heart monitors, insulin pumps, etc.

✓ **Telemedicine platforms** – Remote patient care services.

✓ **Cloud-based systems** – Patient portals, cloud storage, remote access.

✓ **Hospital networks** – Internal Wi-Fi, VPNs, routers, and firewalls.

✓ **Legacy equipment** – Old medical devices that still run Windows XP (yes, that's still a thing).

Each of these is a potential entry point for attackers. Now, let's talk about how they exploit them—and how we stop them.

Common Network Security Threats in Healthcare

1. Ransomware Attacks: The $10 Million "Oops" Moment

Hospitals are prime ransomware targets because they can't afford to be offline. Hackers encrypt patient data and demand a hefty ransom, knowing that hospitals will likely pay rather than risk patient safety.

✓ **Case Study**: In 2020, a German hospital was forced to redirect emergency patients because ransomware shut down critical systems, leading to a patient's death.

🔒 **Defensive Strategy:**

Segment networks to prevent ransomware from spreading.

Back up critical data (offline and offsite).

Use strong endpoint security to detect malware before it executes.

2. Unsecured Medical IoT Devices: The Silent Backdoor

Most connected medical devices weren't designed with security in mind. Many have default passwords, outdated firmware, and zero encryption, making them easy targets.

✓ **Real Threat**: Attackers have demonstrated how to remotely hack pacemakers and alter insulin pump doses.

🔒 **Defensive Strategy:**

Change default passwords on all connected devices.

Isolate medical IoT devices on separate VLANs.

Regularly update firmware (if the manufacturer allows it).

3. Phishing Attacks: When Doctors Click on the Wrong Email

Healthcare workers are busy, and attackers exploit that. Phishing emails disguised as urgent hospital messages trick staff into clicking malicious links—leading to credential theft and malware infections.

✓ **Real Threat**: 91% of ransomware attacks start with phishing.

🔒 **Defensive Strategy:**

Train staff to recognize phishing attempts.

Use multi-factor authentication (MFA) to prevent stolen credential abuse.

Implement email filtering to block malicious links.

4. Weak Wi-Fi and Network Security: The Digital Open Door

Many hospitals still use outdated Wi-Fi encryption (like WEP or WPA1) or leave guest networks wide open. This makes it easy for attackers to eavesdrop on network traffic or launch man-in-the-middle (MITM) attacks.

✓ **Case Study**: A hacker once compromised a hospital's guest Wi-Fi and pivoted into their main network—exposing patient records.

🔒 Defensive Strategy:

Use WPA3 encryption on all hospital Wi-Fi networks.

Separate guest and internal networks with strict firewall rules.

Monitor network traffic for unusual activity.

Hardening Network Security in Hospitals

Now that we know the threats, here's how to lock things down:

1. Implement Network Segmentation

Think of your hospital network like a submarine with watertight compartments—if one part gets breached, the whole system shouldn't go down.

✓ Separate networks for:

Medical IoT devices (infusion pumps, monitors, etc.).

EHR systems and patient databases.

Staff and administrative workstations.

Guest Wi-Fi (never connect this to anything important).

📌 Why? If an attacker compromises one segment, they can't spread laterally to other critical systems.

2. Lock Down Remote Access and VPNs

Remote access is essential for telemedicine and IT management, but poorly secured VPNs are hacker magnets.

✓ Best Practices:

Use multi-factor authentication (MFA) for all remote access.

Block unused VPN accounts (no more "ex-employees" logging in).

Monitor VPN logs for unusual access patterns.

📌 **Why**? Many ransomware attacks start when hackers steal VPN credentials.

3. Use Zero Trust Security (Trust No One, Verify Everything)

Traditional security assumes that once you're inside the network, you're trusted. Bad idea. Zero Trust means:

✓ Every user and device must be verified—constantly.

✓ Access is restricted to only what's necessary.

✓ Devices are continuously monitored for unusual behavior.

📌 **Why**? Even if a hacker steals a password, they shouldn't get full access to everything.

4. Regular Security Audits and Penetration Testing

Hackers test your security for you—so why not beat them to it? Regular penetration testing can:

✓ Find weak points before attackers do.

✓ Expose misconfigurations and vulnerabilities.

✓ Help you fix security gaps proactively.

📌 **Pro Tip**: Conduct red team exercises where ethical hackers simulate attacks to test hospital defenses.

Final Thoughts: Security Isn't Optional in Healthcare

If you're in charge of a hospital's IT security and you haven't checked your firewall rules since 2015, you're playing with fire. Attackers aren't waiting for you to update your systems—they're actively looking for weak spots.

Cybersecurity in healthcare isn't just about protecting data—it's about saving lives. A hacked infusion pump, a compromised EHR system, or a ransomware attack can mean the difference between life and death.

So, here's your final checklist for hardening hospital network security:

✓ **Segment networks** (IoT, patient data, admin, guest Wi-Fi).

✓ **Enforce strong authentication** (MFA, Zero Trust policies).

✓ **Secure Wi-Fi networks** (No WEP, use WPA3).

✓ **Patch and update medical devices** (No excuses).

✓ Train hospital staff to recognize phishing attacks.

✓ Run regular penetration tests (before the hackers do it for you).

Because in the world of healthcare cybersecurity, there are only two types of hospitals:

Those that take security seriously.

Those that have already been hacked.

Which one do you want to be?

Chapter 5: Exploiting Medical IoT Device Vulnerabilities

Imagine a hacker reverse-engineering an insulin pump to deliver a lethal dose remotely. Sounds like a bad sci-fi movie, right? Unfortunately, it's real. Many medical IoT devices ship with hardcoded passwords, outdated firmware, and more security holes than Swiss cheese. And once an attacker finds a way in? Let's just say "malpractice" takes on a whole new meaning.

This chapter dives into the vulnerabilities found in medical IoT devices, including reverse engineering firmware, extracting hardcoded credentials, and exploiting memory corruption issues like buffer overflows. We'll cover real-world attack scenarios and discuss best practices for medical device manufacturers to implement secure coding and firmware development practices to mitigate these risks.

5.1 Reverse Engineering Medical IoT Firmware and Software

Alright, time to put on our hacker goggles and dive deep into the mysterious world of medical IoT firmware and software. If you've ever wondered what makes a pacemaker tick (literally) or how an infusion pump decides to deliver life-saving drugs, you're in the right place.

Reverse engineering medical devices isn't just about poking around in the code for fun—it's about finding vulnerabilities before the bad guys do. Unfortunately, manufacturers don't exactly make this easy. Many medical IoT devices are locked down, with encrypted firmware, proprietary protocols, and legal barriers designed to stop anyone from tinkering.

But here's the harsh reality: hackers don't care about manufacturer restrictions. They're already reverse engineering these devices to find ways to exploit them. If we want to defend medical IoT, we need to understand how they work from the inside out.

So, let's grab some firmware, fire up our disassemblers, and get to work.

Why Reverse Engineer Medical IoT?

Reverse engineering medical IoT firmware serves multiple purposes:

✓ **Finding Vulnerabilities**: Security researchers and ethical hackers look for buffer overflows, hardcoded credentials, and insecure update mechanisms.

✓ **Testing Device Integrity**: Ensure firmware updates aren't compromised by supply chain attacks.

✓ **Interoperability & Customization**: Some developers reverse engineer medical devices to create better third-party integrations.

✓ **Recovering Lost or Unsupported Firmware**: When a manufacturer stops supporting a device, reverse engineering can help keep it running safely.

Of course, attackers also have their own reasons:

⚠ **Exploiting Firmware Backdoors** – Many IoT devices ship with undocumented admin accounts or hardcoded passwords.

⚠ **Modifying Medical Device Behavior** – Imagine an attacker changing the dosage settings on an insulin pump.

⚠ **Extracting Patient Data** – Some devices store sensitive health records in plaintext.

Sounds scary? It is. That's why we need to stay ahead.

Step 1: Extracting Firmware

Before we can analyze anything, we need to get our hands on the firmware. There are three common methods:

1. Download from Manufacturer's Website (The Easy Way)

Some vendors provide firmware publicly as an update file. These are often encrypted, but if not, we can extract the contents easily.

✓ Tools to Use:

binwalk – A powerful tool to analyze and extract firmware images.

strings – Searches for readable text inside the binary (useful for finding credentials).

dd – Helps carve out sections of firmware from larger files.

2. Dumping from the Device's Memory (The Hardware Way)

If the firmware isn't publicly available, we may need to physically extract it using debugging ports or flash memory chips.

✓ Common Interfaces:

JTAG & SWD: Debugging interfaces used for low-level access.

UART & SPI: Serial communication ports that can sometimes leak firmware data.

Flash ROM Extraction: Using a tool like a Bus Pirate or ChipWhisperer to read raw firmware.

🔧 Tools Needed:

JTAGulator – Helps identify JTAG pins on unknown hardware.

Flashrom – Dumps firmware from EEPROM chips.

FTDI Adapters – Connects to serial/UART interfaces.

3. Sniffing Over-the-Air Updates (The Wireless Way)

Some medical IoT devices receive remote firmware updates via Wi-Fi, Bluetooth, or proprietary RF protocols. If updates aren't encrypted (which happens more often than you'd think), attackers can intercept and modify them.

✓ How?

Using Wireshark to capture update packets.

MITM attacks to intercept firmware updates.

Sniffing Bluetooth traffic with tools like HCI Dump or GATTacker.

Step 2: Analyzing and Reverse Engineering the Firmware

Once we have the firmware, it's time to tear it apart and see what's inside.

1. Running Binwalk for Initial Analysis

binwalk -e firmware.bin

This extracts known file types from the binary. Sometimes you'll find hidden files, images, or even plaintext passwords.

2. Looking for Hardcoded Secrets

strings firmware.bin | grep "password"

Many IoT devices store default login credentials in plaintext. Some even leave debugging backdoors open.

3. Disassembling the Code

If we need to dive deeper, we use:

Ghidra – Open-source reverse engineering suite by the NSA.

IDA Pro – Expensive but extremely powerful disassembler.

Radare2 – Free and scriptable alternative to IDA.

At this stage, we're looking for:

Function names and error messages (they reveal a lot).

Encryption routines (to understand how the firmware protects itself).

Potential vulnerabilities (buffer overflows, insecure authentication, etc.).

Step 3: Identifying and Exploiting Vulnerabilities

Now that we've cracked open the firmware, let's look at common security issues we might find.

1. Hardcoded Credentials

One of the worst (and most common) security flaws is when manufacturers hardcode usernames and passwords into the firmware.

✓ **Example:**

char admin_password[] = "mediot_admin_123";

If we find something like this, an attacker could use it to remotely access medical devices.

2. Buffer Overflows

Many medical IoT devices don't perform proper input validation, leading to buffer overflow vulnerabilities.

✓ **Example:**

```
void process_input(char *input) {
    char buffer[32];
    strcpy(buffer, input); // Uh-oh! No bounds checking!
}
```

An attacker could send a specially crafted payload to overflow the buffer and execute malicious code.

3. Insecure Firmware Updates

If a device doesn't verify firmware signatures, an attacker could upload a malicious update and take control of the device.

✓ **Solution:**

Ensure firmware signing is enforced.

Implement secure boot mechanisms.

Defensive Measures: How to Secure Medical IoT Firmware

Now that we've seen how easy it is to exploit weak firmware, let's talk about how to defend against these attacks.

1. Enforce Secure Boot and Signed Firmware

Devices should only accept firmware updates that are cryptographically signed by the manufacturer.

2. Encrypt Stored Data and Credentials

Hardcoded credentials should be eliminated, and sensitive data should be securely encrypted.

3. Implement Firmware Integrity Checks

Medical devices should run checksum or hash verification on their firmware to detect tampering.

4. Regular Security Audits

Manufacturers should conduct regular penetration tests and bug bounty programs to uncover vulnerabilities before attackers do.

Final Thoughts: Reverse Engineering Saves Lives

If we don't reverse engineer medical IoT devices, attackers will. The goal is simple: find the vulnerabilities before the bad guys do, report them, and push manufacturers to fix them.

So next time you see a medical IoT device running outdated firmware, remember—there could be a security flaw hiding inside. And if you're the one to find it, you might just save lives.

Or at the very least, you'll have a fun story to tell at your next hacker meetup. ☺

5.2 Finding and Exploiting Hardcoded Credentials in Medical Devices

Ah, hardcoded credentials—the cybersecurity equivalent of leaving your house keys under the doormat and then posting about it on social media. You'd think in an industry as critical as healthcare, manufacturers would have learned by now that storing passwords inside firmware is a terrible idea. But nope, here we are, still finding default logins hardcoded into medical IoT devices like it's 1999.

In this chapter, we're going to hunt for these security nightmares, break down how attackers find and exploit them, and—most importantly—discuss how to stop this madness before someone gets hurt (literally).

Why Hardcoded Credentials Are a Huge Problem

Hardcoded credentials are login details (usernames, passwords, API keys, etc.) that are baked directly into the firmware or software of a device.

Why is this a problem? Well, once an attacker extracts a device's firmware (which we covered in the previous chapter), they can easily locate these credentials. And since manufacturers often reuse the same credentials across thousands of devices, finding one password can give access to an entire fleet of medical IoT systems.

Imagine a hacker gaining remote admin access to:

Infusion pumps, allowing them to change medication dosages

Pacemakers, where they could disable or manipulate heart rhythms

Medical imaging systems, which store sensitive patient data

Hospital networks, potentially opening the doors for ransomware attacks

Sounds terrifying, right? That's because it is.

Now, let's get our hands dirty and see how attackers find these credentials.

Step 1: Extracting Hardcoded Credentials from Firmware

If a medical device manufacturer has left their passwords inside the firmware, attackers will find them. Here's how they do it:

1. Running Strings Analysis on the Firmware

Once we've extracted the firmware from a medical device (as covered in Chapter 5.1), one of the easiest ways to find passwords is simply searching for readable text inside the binary.

Example Command:

strings firmware.bin | grep -i "password"

💡 What This Does:

Extracts all human-readable text from the firmware.

Looks for any mention of "password" (case insensitive).

✓ Example Output:

admin_password=MedIoTAdmin123
root_password=supersecurepassword
api_key=mediotapikey456

Oops. Looks like we just found some login details.

2. Checking Configuration Files and Scripts

Many medical IoT devices store sensitive credentials inside config files or shell scripts. Attackers look for:

.ini files with default login credentials

Embedded shell scripts that contain authentication tokens

Configuration files (.conf, .xml, .json) with API keys

Example:

grep -i "password" extracted_firmware/etc/.conf*

💡 Why This Works:

Many Linux-based IoT devices store settings in /etc/.

Attackers often find default SSH credentials, database passwords, or API keys here.

Step 2: Disassembling the Binary to Find Hidden Credentials

When passwords aren't stored as plaintext, they may be embedded in the compiled binary code of the firmware.

Using Ghidra or IDA Pro to Reverse Engineer the Binary

✓ Steps:

Load the firmware binary into Ghidra (or IDA Pro)

Search for authentication functions (login, authenticate, check_password)

Look for hardcoded string values inside the function

Example Code Snippet from Disassembly:

char username[] = "medadmin";
char password[] = "HardcodedPass123";

🚨 Found it! Now an attacker knows exactly what credentials to use.

Step 3: Exploiting Hardcoded Credentials

Now that we have default usernames and passwords, let's see how an attacker would use them.

1. SSH or Telnet Access

Many medical IoT devices expose SSH or Telnet ports for remote management. If they're using hardcoded credentials, an attacker just needs to connect using the username and password found in the firmware.

Example Attack:

ssh mediotadmin@hospitaldevice.local

Once inside, an attacker can:

✓ Modify device settings

✓ Steal patient data

✓ Inject malware or ransomware

2. Web-Based Admin Panels

Some medical IoT devices come with web interfaces where administrators can log in. Attackers can simply try the hardcoded credentials in the login page.

✓ How Attackers Find Web Panels:

nmap -p 80,443 --open -sV hospitalnetwork.local

✓ Example Login:

URL: http://hospitaldevice.local/admin

Username: admin

Password: defaultpass123

💀 Boom, they're in.

3. Exploiting API Keys for Remote Attacks

Some medical devices communicate with cloud services using hardcoded API keys. If attackers find these keys, they can impersonate the device and:

✓ Steal patient records

✓ Send malicious commands to medical devices

✓ Disable security updates

Example API Call Using Stolen Key:

```
curl -H "Authorization: Bearer mediotapikey456" https://hospitalapi.com/getRecords
```

✓ Patient data exposed. Just like that.

Defensive Measures: How to Prevent Hardcoded Credentials

Okay, so how do we fix this disaster?

1. Use Secure Authentication Methods

✓ Implement dynamic authentication instead of static hardcoded passwords.

✓ Require multi-factor authentication (MFA) for access.

2. Encrypt Stored Credentials Properly

✓ Store credentials securely in a separate encrypted storage, not inside the firmware.

✓ Use environment variables instead of hardcoded values.

3. Enforce Unique Per-Device Credentials

✓ Every device should have a unique password generated during setup.

✓ Use device certificates instead of static passwords.

4. Regular Security Audits & Penetration Testing

✓ Manufacturers must conduct routine security audits to detect hardcoded credentials.

✓ Hospitals should scan devices for known weak credentials using tools like:

nmap --script http-default-accounts

hydra for brute-force testing

Final Thoughts: Don't Be the Next Headline

Finding hardcoded credentials in medical IoT devices is embarrassingly common. Attackers know it, and now (hopefully) you do too. If you take nothing else from this chapter, remember:

Hardcoded passwords are a terrible idea.

Attackers will find them.

And when they do, bad things happen.

If we don't start fixing these security flaws now, we're going to see more cases where hackers take control of life-saving devices. And that's not just a security risk—it's a matter of life and death.

So, let's do better. Otherwise, I'll have to keep writing chapters like this, and frankly, I'd rather not. ☺

5.3 Memory Corruption Attacks (Buffer Overflows, Heap Exploits)

Alright, let's talk about memory corruption attacks—the cybersecurity equivalent of crashing a hospital's IT system by shoving too many snacks into a vending machine. Except in this case, the vending machine is a medical IoT device, and the snacks are malicious inputs designed to break the system.

If you've ever heard of a buffer overflow or heap exploit, you know these aren't just theoretical attacks. They're real, nasty, and shockingly common in legacy medical devices. Why? Because a lot of these devices were never designed with cybersecurity in mind. They were built to keep patients alive—not to defend against someone stuffing their input fields with 10,000 "A" characters.

So, in this chapter, we'll break down what memory corruption attacks are, how attackers exploit them, and—most importantly—how we can defend against them before someone accidentally (or intentionally) bricks a ventilator.

What Is a Memory Corruption Attack?

A memory corruption attack occurs when an attacker manipulates a system's memory in ways it wasn't designed to handle. This can lead to:

✓ System crashes (Denial-of-Service attacks)

✓ Execution of malicious code (Remote Code Execution)

✓ Privilege escalation (Gaining admin control over a device)

Since many medical IoT devices run on embedded Linux, RTOS, or outdated C/C++ applications, they're often vulnerable to classic memory corruption exploits like:

Buffer Overflows: Overwriting adjacent memory to execute arbitrary code.

Heap Exploits: Manipulating memory allocation to corrupt critical data.

Format String Attacks: Abusing unchecked input formatting to leak or overwrite data.

Buffer Overflows: The Classic Memory Attack

Imagine a hospital receptionist only has 20 slots in their appointment book, but you show up with 200 names. They try to write all of them down, but—oops!—they spill over onto other critical pages (like the administrator's login info).

That's a buffer overflow in a nutshell.

Medical IoT devices often have poor input validation, meaning an attacker can send more data than expected, overflowing the buffer and overwriting nearby memory.

Example of a Simple Buffer Overflow in C

Many legacy medical IoT devices still run C-based software with poor memory protection.

```
#include <stdio.h>
#include <string.h>

void vulnerable_function(char *input) {
    char buffer[50];  // Small buffer
    strcpy(buffer, input);  // No bounds checking
    printf("Received: %s\n", buffer);
}
```

```
int main(int argc, char *argv[]) {
    vulnerable_function(argv[1]);
    return 0;
}
```

Exploiting This Vulnerability

An attacker could run the program like this:

./meddevice `python3 -c 'print("A"*100)'`

Since strcpy() doesn't check input size, it will overwrite the return address, potentially allowing the attacker to execute malicious code.

Heap Exploits: Messing with Dynamic Memory Allocation

While buffer overflows target fixed-size memory buffers, heap exploits manipulate dynamically allocated memory to corrupt adjacent structures or gain control over function pointers.

How Heap Exploits Work in Medical IoT

Many medical applications use dynamic memory allocation (like malloc() and free()). If an attacker crafts input to mess with how memory is allocated or freed, they can:

✓ Corrupt sensitive medical data (e.g., alter patient records in RAM)

✓ Redirect execution flow to malicious code

✓ Bypass access control

Example Heap Exploit

Consider a medical data logging system that dynamically allocates memory for patient records:

```
#include <stdio.h>
#include <stdlib.h>
#include <string.h>
```

```
struct Patient {
    char name[32];
    int age;
};

void process_patient(char *name) {
    struct Patient *p = malloc(sizeof(struct Patient));
    strcpy(p->name, name);  // No bounds checking
    printf("Processing patient: %s\n", p->name);
    free(p);
}

int main(int argc, char *argv[]) {
    process_patient(argv[1]);
    return 0;
}
```

An attacker could overflow the heap and overwrite function pointers or return addresses, gaining control over the execution flow.

Real-World Memory Corruption Attacks in Healthcare

Memory corruption vulnerabilities aren't just theoretical risks—they've already been exploited in real-world medical environments.

Case Study 1: Infusion Pump Exploit

💻 Security researchers found a buffer overflow vulnerability in a widely used infusion pump. Attackers could send malformed data packets, causing the device to execute arbitrary commands, potentially changing medication dosages.

Case Study 2: MRI Machine Remote Exploit

💻 A hospital's MRI machine was found vulnerable to heap-based exploits. Attackers could manipulate its image processing software, leading to data corruption or even backdoor access to hospital networks.

How to Defend Against Memory Corruption Attacks

Alright, enough doom and gloom. Let's talk defense strategies.

1. Use Memory-Safe Programming Languages

C and C++ are notorious for memory vulnerabilities. Consider using:

✓ **Rust** (Memory safety without performance trade-offs)

✓ **Go** (Garbage-collected and safer than C)

✓ **Python** (Not always feasible, but avoids direct memory manipulation)

2. Enable Compiler Protections

Modern compilers provide built-in security features to mitigate memory corruption risks:

✓ **Stack Canaries** (-fstack-protector in GCC)

✓ **Address Space Layout Randomization** (ASLR) (execstack -c)

✓ **Fortify Source** (-D_FORTIFY_SOURCE=2)

3. Implement Proper Input Validation

✓ Use strncpy() instead of strcpy()

✓ Use safe memory functions like memcpy_s()

✓ Sanitize all user inputs before processing

4. Conduct Regular Security Audits

✓ Fuzz Testing: Identify vulnerabilities by sending random data

✓ Static Code Analysis: Detect memory corruption bugs early

✓ Penetration Testing: Simulate attacks on medical devices

Final Thoughts: Memory Safety is Patient Safety

Medical IoT devices aren't just computers—they're lifesaving machines. A single buffer overflow or heap exploit could mean the difference between life and death. If manufacturers and hospitals don't take memory safety seriously, attackers will gladly take advantage.

So, let's fix these issues before a hacker decides to do it for us. Because honestly, if I have to write another chapter about "How Hackers Can Kill You with a Segmentation Fault", I might just throw my laptop out the window. ☺

5.4 Remote Code Execution (RCE) on Smart Medical Devices

You ever wake up in a cold sweat thinking, What if someone hacks my pacemaker while I'm asleep? No? Just me? Cool.

Welcome to the terrifying world of Remote Code Execution (RCE) on medical IoT devices, where hackers can remotely take control of critical healthcare equipment, from infusion pumps to MRI machines. Unlike your grandma accidentally downloading malware on her laptop, RCE on medical devices isn't just an inconvenience—it's a literal life-or-death situation.

In this chapter, we'll break down what RCE attacks are, how attackers exploit vulnerabilities in medical IoT devices, and most importantly, how we can stop them before a cybercriminal decides to play doctor.

What is Remote Code Execution (RCE)?

Remote Code Execution (RCE) is the holy grail of hacking—it allows an attacker to run any code they want on a target system, from anywhere in the world.

For a hacker, an RCE vulnerability on a smart medical device is like getting admin access to the human body. It means they can:

✓ **Modify device behavior** (e.g., change drug dosages on an infusion pump)

✓ **Install malware or ransomware** (locking down critical hospital equipment)

✓ **Extract sensitive patient data** (PHI = $$$ on the dark web)

✓ **Turn devices into botnets** (because even pacemakers can mine crypto now)

Medical IoT devices are especially vulnerable because many of them:

Run on outdated or unpatched operating systems

Use default or hardcoded credentials

Have weak network security

Were never designed with cybersecurity in mind

Let's look at how attackers actually pull off RCE attacks on medical IoT.

Common RCE Attack Vectors in Medical IoT

RCE doesn't happen by magic (though it might seem that way). Attackers exploit specific vulnerabilities in software, firmware, and network configurations to execute their code.

1. Exploiting Buffer Overflows & Memory Corruption

Remember that buffer overflow attack we talked about earlier? That's a classic RCE technique. If an attacker can overwrite return addresses or function pointers, they can redirect execution to their malicious payload.

✅ **Example**: A researcher found an RCE vulnerability in a hospital's MRI machine, allowing them to execute arbitrary code by exploiting a heap overflow in the image processing software.

2. Attacking Unauthenticated Web Interfaces & APIs

Many smart medical devices expose web interfaces or REST APIs for configuration and remote monitoring. If these lack authentication or input validation, attackers can inject malicious commands.

✅ **Example**: A widely used insulin pump was found to have an exposed API endpoint that accepted unauthenticated POST requests. This allowed attackers to remotely change insulin delivery settings—a literal life-threatening vulnerability.

3. Command Injection in Embedded Firmware

If a device accepts user-controlled input and passes it directly to system commands without proper sanitization, attackers can execute commands as root.

✓ **Example**: An X-ray machine was found to be vulnerable to command injection. By sending a maliciously crafted request through its network interface, researchers gained full control over the device, including the ability to disable safety checks.

4. Exploiting Hardcoded Credentials and Backdoors

A shockingly high number of medical IoT devices ship with hardcoded admin credentials. If these are exposed, attackers can log in remotely and execute arbitrary commands.

✓ **Example**: A hospital's remote patient monitoring system had a hardcoded "admin:admin" login. Attackers could remotely log in, execute shell commands, and install backdoors for persistent access.

Real-World RCE Attacks in Healthcare

Case Study 1: Infusion Pump Takeover

💻 Security researchers discovered an RCE vulnerability in a widely used infusion pump. Attackers could exploit a flaw in the pump's firmware update mechanism, allowing them to remotely install malicious software. This meant they could increase, decrease, or stop drug dosages altogether.

Case Study 2: MRI Machines Used for Cryptojacking

💻 A hospital's MRI scanner network was hacked and turned into a cryptocurrency mining farm. Attackers exploited an RCE vulnerability in the scanner's remote access feature, using it to install crypto-mining malware—slowing down the machines and delaying patient scans.

Case Study 3: Ransomware on Hospital Imaging Systems

💻 Attackers exploited an RCE vulnerability in a hospital's radiology software. They deployed ransomware, locking all patient imaging files until a ransom was paid.

Defending Against RCE Attacks in Medical IoT

Alright, now that we're all sufficiently terrified, let's talk defense. Here's how to stop RCE attacks before they turn your hospital into a hacker's playground.

1. Patch and Update Everything (Yes, Everything)

✓ Apply security updates ASAP (No excuses!)

✓ Upgrade legacy medical devices or isolate them from the internet

✓ Regularly check vendor advisories for new vulnerabilities

2. Implement Strong Authentication & Access Controls

✓ Disable default admin credentials

✓ Require multi-factor authentication (MFA) for remote access

✓ Restrict device access to authorized personnel only

3. Secure Medical Device APIs and Web Interfaces

✓ Use authentication tokens (No unauthenticated API calls!)

✓ Sanitize all user inputs (No command injections!)

✓ Disable unnecessary features in production

4. Harden Device Firmware & Operating Systems

✓ Enable Address Space Layout Randomization (ASLR)

✓ Use Stack Canaries to prevent buffer overflows

✓ Implement code signing to prevent unauthorized firmware updates

5. Network Segmentation & Firewall Rules

✓ Separate medical IoT devices from the hospital's main IT network

✓ Use firewalls and intrusion detection to block suspicious traffic

✓ Disable unnecessary remote access services

Final Thoughts: Your Smart Pacemaker Shouldn't Be a Cybercrime Tool

At the end of the day, medical IoT devices are supposed to save lives—not be remotely hijacked by hackers for fun and profit. RCE vulnerabilities aren't just an IT problem—they're a patient safety crisis.

If manufacturers don't start taking cybersecurity seriously, we're going to see more hospitals paying ransoms, more patient data leaks, and worst of all, more life-threatening cyberattacks.

So, let's fix this before we end up with a Netflix documentary titled "When Hackers Kill: The Medical IoT Disaster". 🚨

5.5 Implementing Secure Coding Practices for Medical IoT Development

Let's be honest—most medical IoT devices are held together by duct tape, legacy code, and a prayer. Somewhere out there, a pacemaker is running on software that hasn't been updated since flip phones were cool. And if that doesn't terrify you, consider this: a single coding flaw in a smart insulin pump could turn lifesaving technology into a deadly weapon.

Welcome to the wild world of secure coding for medical IoT—where one bad buffer overflow can put lives, hospitals, and entire healthcare systems at risk. In this chapter, we'll dive into the best practices for writing secure code, how to avoid common pitfalls, and how to keep hackers from turning your medical device into a botnet for mining cryptocurrency.

The High Stakes of Insecure Code in Medical IoT

Most security vulnerabilities in medical IoT devices start at the code level. A poorly written firmware update can introduce hardcoded credentials. A lack of proper input validation can lead to remote code execution (RCE). And if a developer isn't paying attention, a single unpatched bug can allow attackers to change drug dosages, disable life-support systems, or extract patient health data.

Here's why secure coding matters:

✓ **Patients' lives are at risk** – A compromised pacemaker or infusion pump isn't just an IT problem; it's a life-threatening event.

✓ **Hospitals are prime ransomware targets** – One unsecured API can lead to an entire hospital being locked down by cybercriminals demanding millions in Bitcoin.

✓ **Regulatory fines are brutal** – A data breach involving protected health information (PHI) means HIPAA, FDA, and GDPR violations, leading to massive lawsuits and penalties.

So how do we fix this mess? By writing medical IoT software like lives depend on it—because they do.

Secure Coding Principles for Medical IoT

1. Secure by Design (Start Strong, Stay Strong)

Security shouldn't be an afterthought. It needs to be baked into the development lifecycle from day one. Follow Secure by Design principles to reduce vulnerabilities before they make it into production.

✓ Use threat modeling early in development.

✓ Follow least privilege—never give more permissions than necessary.

✓ Implement code review processes with security in mind.

🔒 **Bad Example**: A hospital's heart monitor software was designed with an open telnet port for easy debugging. The manufacturer forgot to disable it before release. Hackers found it. Chaos ensued.

2. Avoid Hardcoded Credentials (Seriously, Just Stop)

One of the biggest mistakes developers make is embedding usernames and passwords directly into the firmware. If attackers find them, game over—they have permanent backdoor access.

✔ **Better Practice**: Use secure credential storage and implement proper authentication mechanisms like OAuth or certificate-based authentication.

🔒 **Real-World Fail**: A smart insulin pump was found to have hardcoded admin credentials ("admin:1234"), allowing attackers to remotely change insulin doses.

3. Implement Strong Input Validation (Sanitize Everything!)

Never trust user input. EVER. Attackers love injecting malicious code through poorly validated inputs, leading to command injection, SQL injection, and RCE attacks.

✓ Sanitize all user inputs—block unexpected characters.

✓ Use parameterized queries instead of string concatenation for SQL.

✓ Limit input length to prevent buffer overflow attacks.

⚖ **Worst Case Scenario**: A wireless drug infusion pump accepted user input without validation. Hackers sent a malicious payload that caused the pump to increase drug dosage to fatal levels.

4. Secure Firmware Updates (Because Hackers Love Old Code)

Medical devices often run outdated software, making them prime targets for exploits that were patched years ago. Implementing secure firmware updates is critical to keeping devices safe.

✅ Best Practices for Secure Firmware Updates:

✓ Use cryptographic signing to prevent tampered updates.

✓ Require device authentication before applying updates.

✓ Implement rollback protection to prevent attackers from installing old, vulnerable firmware.

⚖ **Case Study**: A hospital MRI scanner had an unsecured update process. Attackers replaced the firmware with malware, allowing them to exfiltrate patient scans and hold them for ransom.

5. Enforce Strong API Security (No Open Endpoints!)

APIs are the backbone of connected healthcare, allowing medical IoT devices to communicate with cloud services, hospitals, and mobile apps. But if APIs aren't secured, attackers can steal data, inject malicious commands, or hijack devices remotely.

✅ **API Security Best Practices:**

✓ Require authentication and authorization for every API request.

✓ Use rate limiting to prevent brute-force attacks.

✓ Encrypt all API communications with TLS 1.2+.

🚨 **Real-World Example**: A telemedicine platform exposed an unauthenticated API that allowed anyone to access patient records. Hackers scraped thousands of medical histories before the issue was discovered.

Building a Culture of Secure Coding in Medical IoT

Secure coding isn't just about following best practices—it's about creating a security-first mindset in your development team. Here's how:

✓ Train developers on secure coding practices. (No one is born knowing how to prevent RCE.)

✓ Conduct regular security audits. (Find vulnerabilities before attackers do.)

✓ Use automated security testing tools. (Because manual testing alone isn't enough.)

✓ Encourage responsible disclosure. (Bug bounty programs can help!)

Final Thoughts: Write Code Like Lives Depend on It (Because They Do)

Let's be real—bad code in a social media app might expose your selfies. Bad code in a pacemaker can kill people.

If we want secure, hacker-resistant medical IoT devices, we need to start at the source: the code itself. That means no hardcoded passwords, no sloppy API security, no unpatched firmware, and no trusting user input like it's your best friend.

Secure coding isn't optional in medical IoT. It's the difference between a patient surviving surgery and a hacker taking control of a ventilator for fun. Let's do better.

And hey—if you ever find yourself tempted to take a shortcut in security because "no one will notice," just remember: hackers always notice. 🚨

Chapter 6: Wireless Attacks on Smart Healthcare Devices

Wireless medical devices are amazing—until someone hijacks them. Imagine a hacker jamming a wireless pacemaker or replaying signals to an insulin pump. It's like an invisible attack, with no physical access needed. And because hospitals love using outdated wireless protocols, breaking into these systems is often easier than guessing your grandparents' Wi-Fi password (which, let's be honest, is probably just "password").

In this chapter, we explore wireless vulnerabilities in healthcare environments, covering attacks on Bluetooth, BLE, NFC, Zigbee, RFID, and Wi-Fi-connected medical devices. We'll discuss sniffing, replay attacks, jamming techniques, and the risks of using unpatched wireless protocols in medical settings. Securing wireless communications is a crucial step in protecting patient safety and data integrity.

6.1 Bluetooth and BLE Exploits in Wearable Health Devices

Bluetooth is that one friend who's fun to have around but constantly forgets to lock their door. It's everywhere—from your wireless earbuds to smart fridges—and, unfortunately, medical IoT devices. Wearable health devices like fitness trackers, smartwatches, glucose monitors, and heart rate sensors rely on Bluetooth and Bluetooth Low Energy (BLE) for data transmission. But here's the problem: most Bluetooth security measures are as weak as hospital Wi-Fi passwords (which, let's be honest, are usually just "hospital123").

In this chapter, we'll explore how attackers can exploit Bluetooth and BLE vulnerabilities to steal health data, manipulate device readings, and even take control of wearable medical devices. More importantly, we'll discuss how to defend against these attacks before someone turns your smart insulin pump into a remote-controlled weapon.

Bluetooth and BLE: A Hacker's Playground

Bluetooth has been around since the '90s, and while it's evolved, security has always been an afterthought. BLE, a low-power variant of Bluetooth, is particularly popular in wearable health devices because it extends battery life. But here's the catch—it sacrifices security for efficiency.

Common security issues in Bluetooth and BLE medical devices include:

✓ **Weak pairing mechanisms** – Many devices still use default or predictable PINs (0000 or 1234, anyone?).

✓ **Lack of authentication** – Some wearables automatically connect to any nearby Bluetooth device without verifying its identity.

✓ **Unencrypted data transmission** – Attackers can easily intercept medical data if it's sent in plaintext.

✓ **Insecure firmware updates** – Some devices don't verify updates, making them vulnerable to malicious firmware injections.

🚨 **Real-World Fail:**

In 2018, researchers found that many Bluetooth-enabled glucose monitors could be hijacked remotely. Attackers could alter blood sugar readings, tricking patients into taking incorrect doses of insulin. Scary, right?

Common Bluetooth & BLE Exploits in Medical IoT

1. Sniffing & Eavesdropping Attacks

Most Bluetooth devices broadcast their presence to connect with other devices. This makes Bluetooth sniffing a breeze. Using tools like Ubertooth One, attackers can:

✓ Capture unencrypted medical data from wearables.

✓ Identify device vulnerabilities and possible entry points.

✓ Replay intercepted packets to manipulate device behavior.

🚨 **Example Attack**: A hacker sitting in a hospital lobby sniffs real-time ECG data from patients' Bluetooth-enabled heart monitors.

2. MITM (Man-in-the-Middle) Attacks

In a MITM attack, an attacker intercepts communication between a wearable device and its paired smartphone or cloud service.

✓ Intercept health data and modify it before it reaches the app.

✓ Inject malicious commands into the device (e.g., triggering an overdose in an insulin pump).

✓ Use cloned devices to impersonate a legitimate medical wearable.

🔍 **Example Attack**: An attacker uses BtleJuice to intercept and modify blood pressure readings before they appear on a doctor's tablet, leading to incorrect diagnoses.

3. Replay Attacks

In a replay attack, hackers capture a legitimate Bluetooth communication and resend it later to trigger unauthorized actions.

✓ Override a previous valid command (e.g., adjusting medication dosage).

✓ Bypass authentication by replaying old connection requests.

✓ Trigger false alarms or alerts in medical monitoring systems.

🔍 **Example Attack**: A hacker records a command that instructs a wearable drug delivery device to dispense medication, then replays it later, leading to a dangerous overdose.

4. Bluetooth Impersonation & Spoofing

Some Bluetooth devices don't properly verify who they're connecting to. Attackers can spoof trusted devices and trick medical wearables into:

✓ Sending data to a malicious device instead of the intended recipient.

✓ Pairing with an unauthorized device, allowing full control.

✓ Receiving malicious firmware updates from an attacker-controlled source.

🔍 **Example Attack**: A hacker sets up a fake "doctor's tablet" that tricks pacemakers into sending sensitive health data to an attacker instead of the hospital system.

Defensive Strategies: How to Secure Bluetooth in Medical IoT

Now that we've sufficiently scared you, let's talk about how to defend against these attacks.

1. Enforce Strong Authentication & Pairing

✓ **Ditch default PINs** – Make devices require strong authentication instead of relying on 0000 or 1234.

✓ **Use passkey confirmation** – Ensure users confirm pairing requests instead of blindly accepting them.

✓ Enable two-factor authentication (2FA) for wearables that connect to cloud services.

2. Encrypt Bluetooth Communications

✓ Use Bluetooth Secure Simple Pairing (SSP) with encryption enabled.

✓ Disable plaintext data transmission—all data should be encrypted with strong cryptographic algorithms.

✓ Use TLS encryption for cloud-connected Bluetooth devices.

3. Implement Secure Firmware Updates

✓ Digitally sign firmware updates to prevent malicious code injection.

✓ Require user confirmation before applying updates.

✓ Disable Bluetooth-based updates unless absolutely necessary.

4. Restrict Bluetooth Signal Range & Discovery Mode

✓ Disable Bluetooth discovery mode when not in use to prevent unauthorized pairing.

✓ Reduce Bluetooth transmission power so signals don't leak beyond intended areas (like hospital rooms).

5. Monitor & Log Bluetooth Connections

✓ Detect unauthorized pairing attempts in real time.

✓ Alert administrators if a device connects to an unknown Bluetooth device.

✓ Regularly audit Bluetooth logs to spot anomalies.

Final Thoughts: Bluetooth Security Shouldn't Be an Afterthought

Bluetooth in medical IoT is both a blessing and a curse. On one hand, it enables life-changing wearable health devices. On the other hand, it introduces serious security risks that can put patient lives in danger.

As security professionals, we can't afford to ignore these vulnerabilities. If attackers can take over a smartwatch, they can just as easily hijack a wearable drug delivery system.

So next time you see a Bluetooth-enabled pacemaker or insulin pump, ask yourself:

🚨 Did the developers actually secure this thing, or did they just hope no one would notice? 🚨

Because hackers always notice.

6.2 Sniffing and Manipulating NFC-Based Medical Transactions

If Bluetooth is the forgetful friend who leaves their door unlocked, NFC (Near Field Communication) is the friend who hands their house keys to complete strangers, assuming they look trustworthy. NFC is everywhere in modern healthcare—from patient check-ins to smart insulin pens—but here's the kicker: most people assume it's secure just because it has a short range. Spoiler alert: it's not.

In this chapter, we'll explore how attackers can sniff, clone, and manipulate NFC-based medical transactions, steal patient data, and even alter medication administration records—all without even touching the victim's device. And because NFC security is often overlooked, many hospitals and medical device manufacturers have left some pretty wide doors open for attackers. Buckle up!

What is NFC, and Why is It Used in Healthcare?

Near Field Communication (NFC) is a short-range wireless technology that allows two devices to communicate when they are within a few centimeters of each other. You've probably used NFC for contactless payments, keyless entry, or scanning a smart tag at a store.

In healthcare, NFC is used for:

✓ **Patient Identification & Check-in** – Hospitals use NFC wristbands or ID cards to identify patients and update medical records.

✓ **Medication Dispensing** – Smart insulin pens and pill dispensers use NFC to track medication usage.

✓ **Medical Equipment Authentication** – Some NFC-enabled medical devices authenticate users before allowing operation.

✓ **Access Control** – Doctors and nurses use NFC badges to access restricted hospital areas or retrieve patient records.

NFC sounds secure because of its short range (usually under 10 cm), but attackers have ways of sniffing, intercepting, and manipulating NFC transactions without needing direct physical access.

Common NFC-Based Attacks in Medical IoT

1. NFC Sniffing Attacks

Most NFC communications are not encrypted, which means that attackers with the right equipment can eavesdrop on NFC transactions. Using devices like Proxmark3, attackers can:

✓ Capture patient information from an NFC hospital wristband.

✓ Intercept medical payment transactions at a hospital's self-check-in kiosk.

✓ Steal authentication tokens from NFC-enabled medical staff ID badges.

🔍 **Example Attack**: An attacker sits in a hospital waiting room with an NFC sniffer and quietly captures patient check-in details from unsuspecting visitors' wristbands.

2. NFC Relay Attacks

NFC's short range should protect it, right? Well, not if hackers use a relay attack. In this attack, an attacker relays NFC signals between a legitimate device and a faraway attacker, tricking the system into thinking the real device is nearby.

✓ **Bypass hospital access control** – A hacker standing outside the hospital relays an NFC badge's signal to an accomplice inside, who now has full access.

✓ **Exploit smart drug dispensers** – A patient's NFC-enabled insulin pen could be remotely triggered to inject the wrong dosage.

✓ **Tamper with patient identification** – By relaying an NFC wristband's signal, an attacker could check in as someone else.

🔎 **Example Attack**: A hacker in a parking lot relays a doctor's NFC badge signal to an attacker inside the hospital, who gains access to restricted patient records.

3. NFC Cloning & Replay Attacks

Some NFC-based systems don't verify if an NFC tag is genuine or copied. Using cloning tools, attackers can:

✓ Duplicate patient wristbands to gain unauthorized access to medical services.

✓ Copy an NFC medical badge and use it to impersonate a doctor.

✓ Replay NFC medication transactions to make it appear as if a patient took their meds when they didn't.

🔎 **Example Attack**: A hacker clones a patient's NFC hospital wristband and uses it to steal their medical prescription at a pharmacy.

4. Malicious NFC Tags (NFC Exploits in Smartphones)

Attackers can create malicious NFC tags that, when scanned, trigger malware downloads, phishing links, or unauthorized transactions.

✓ Infect a doctor's smartphone by leaving an infected NFC tag near a hospital workstation.

✓ Redirect medical staff to a phishing site that looks like the hospital's internal system.

✓ Inject malicious code into NFC-enabled medical apps.

🔎 **Example Attack**: An attacker leaves a malicious NFC sticker near a hospital's self-check-in kiosk, redirecting patients to a fake login page to steal their medical records.

Defensive Strategies: Securing NFC in Medical IoT

1. Encrypt NFC Communications

✓ Enable encryption for NFC-based patient data transactions.

✓ Use secure authentication protocols before allowing NFC interactions.

✓ Disable NFC when not in use to prevent passive scanning attacks.

2. Implement Strong Authentication

✓ Require PINs or biometric authentication before approving NFC-based medical transactions.

✓ Ensure two-factor authentication (2FA) for NFC-based hospital access control.

✓ Use dynamic NFC tags that change with each interaction to prevent replay attacks.

3. Secure NFC Medical Devices

✓ Restrict NFC device pairing to authorized systems only.

✓ Regularly audit NFC access logs to detect anomalies.

✓ Use anti-tampering NFC stickers to prevent unauthorized cloning.

4. Prevent NFC Relay & Cloning Attacks

✓ Implement time-sensitive transactions that expire quickly.

✓ Use physical NFC shields to block signal relaying.

✓ Deploy NFC challenge-response authentication to verify authenticity.

Final Thoughts: Don't Trust NFC Just Because It's "Close-Range"

Many hospitals assume NFC is secure just because it has a short range—but that's a dangerous assumption. Attackers don't need to physically touch NFC devices to clone, relay, or manipulate transactions.

So next time you tap your hospital NFC badge or scan an NFC-powered insulin pen, ask yourself:

🔍 Is this actually secure, or am I just hoping no one's watching? 🔍

Because hackers are always watching—sometimes from the hospital waiting room.

6.3 Jamming and Replay Attacks on Wireless Infusion Pumps

Ah, wireless infusion pumps—the unsung heroes of modern hospitals. These magical little machines deliver precise doses of medication to patients, saving lives one carefully measured drip at a time. But what happens when a hacker decides to mess with that precision? Well, let's just say things get dangerous very quickly.

In this chapter, we'll explore how attackers can jam the wireless signals controlling these pumps, replay old commands, and even manipulate medication dosages without ever touching the device. If you thought "accidentally drinking expired milk" was a bad mistake, imagine getting a double dose of morphine because a hacker decided to play DJ with your medication schedule.

The Role of Wireless Infusion Pumps in Healthcare

Before we dive into the scary security risks, let's appreciate why wireless infusion pumps have become so popular in hospitals:

✓ **Remote Monitoring & Control** – Nurses can adjust medication dosages without entering a patient's room.

✓ **Automated Drug Delivery** – The system ensures consistent medication administration without human error.

✓ **Integration with EHR Systems** – Infusion pumps connect to Electronic Health Records (EHRs) for real-time data logging.

✓ **Reduced Workload for Medical Staff** – Automation means less manual intervention, allowing staff to focus on critical care.

Sounds amazing, right? Until you realize these devices can be hijacked just like your Wi-Fi router.

Jamming Attacks on Wireless Infusion Pumps

How Jamming Attacks Work

Wireless infusion pumps rely on Wi-Fi, Bluetooth, or Zigbee to receive instructions. If an attacker floods these signals with interference, the pumps stop receiving commands—or worse, they might start acting unpredictably.

A hacker with a simple radio frequency (RF) jammer can:

✓ Block remote commands, forcing nurses to enter medication manually.

✓ Disrupt medication schedules, delaying life-saving treatments.

✓ Cause system-wide failures, affecting multiple patients in a hospital ward.

🔊 **Example Attack**: A hacker hides a portable jammer in a hospital waiting room. Suddenly, all infusion pumps in the ICU lose connectivity, forcing nurses to scramble and manually enter medication doses.

Why Jamming is Dangerous in Healthcare

Unlike your annoying neighbor messing with your Wi-Fi, jamming a medical device isn't just an inconvenience—it's life-threatening. Patients rely on wireless infusion pumps for everything from pain management to chemotherapy drugs, and disrupting that process can have catastrophic consequences.

Replay Attacks: The Danger of "Replaying" Old Commands

What is a Replay Attack?

A replay attack is when a hacker captures a legitimate command (like a nurse adjusting an infusion pump) and replays it later—even when it's no longer needed.

An attacker can:

✓ Re-send an old dosage command, causing an overdose.

✓ Replay a "stop medication" command, cutting off life-saving drugs.

✓ Trick the system into thinking medication was administered when it wasn't.

🔔 **Example Attack**: A hacker records a legitimate command that sets a patient's insulin pump to deliver 4 units of insulin. Hours later, they replay the same command multiple times, sending the patient into a hypoglycemic shock.

Why Wireless Infusion Pumps Are Vulnerable

Many older wireless infusion pumps lack proper encryption or authentication, meaning they blindly accept commands as long as they "look" valid. Attackers don't even need to know how the device works—they just need to capture and replay signals until something breaks.

Case Studies: Real-World Infusion Pump Attacks

1. The 2017 FDA Infusion Pump Warning

In 2017, the FDA issued a warning about a widely used infusion pump model that could be remotely hijacked due to weak security protections. The vulnerability allowed attackers to:

✓ Change infusion rates remotely

✓ Override medication settings

✓ Turn the pump off entirely

The manufacturer had to release emergency patches, but many hospitals were slow to update—leaving patients vulnerable for months.

2. Black Hat Conference: Hacking Infusion Pumps Live

At Black Hat 2018, security researchers demonstrated live how they could take control of an infusion pump, alter medication dosages, and even disable alarms—all remotely.

Their findings showed that:

✓ Many infusion pumps still use default passwords.

✓ Some models have no encryption for wireless commands.

✓ Replay attacks work because devices don't verify timestamps.

Defensive Strategies: How to Protect Infusion Pumps from Attackers

1. Encrypt Wireless Communications

✓ Use end-to-end encryption to prevent unauthorized sniffing of commands.

✓ Ensure devices authenticate commands before executing them.

✓ Regularly update firmware to patch known vulnerabilities.

2. Implement Secure Authentication

✓ Use two-factor authentication (2FA) for remote pump access.

✓ Require unique cryptographic keys for each device.

✓ Disable unused wireless communication protocols.

3. Prevent Jamming Attacks

✓ Use frequency-hopping spread spectrum (FHSS) to make signals harder to jam.

✓ Deploy RF monitoring tools to detect unusual interference.

✓ Shield critical areas of hospitals from external RF attacks.

4. Stop Replay Attacks

✓ Use time-sensitive tokens to prevent old commands from being replayed.

✓ Ensure that every command is digitally signed and verified.

✓ Implement logging and anomaly detection to flag suspicious activity.

Final Thoughts: Are Hackers Controlling Your Medication?

The idea that someone outside the hospital could remotely change your medication dosage is terrifying—but it's not science fiction. Wireless infusion pumps offer incredible convenience, but without proper security, they're ticking time bombs.

So next time you see a nurse adjusting a patient's infusion pump wirelessly, ask yourself:

🔘 Is this safe? Or could some random hacker be replaying an old command right now? 🔘

Because in the world of medical IoT security, the scariest threats are often the ones you can't see—but can definitely feel.

6.4 Exploiting Zigbee and RFID in Smart Hospital Systems

Hospitals today are packed with fancy smart systems—automated patient tracking, medication dispensing, and even smart beds that adjust themselves (because getting comfortable in a hospital bed is apparently a high-tech problem). But behind all this cool innovation lurks a security nightmare: Zigbee and RFID.

These two wireless technologies power many critical hospital operations, but guess what? They're also ridiculously easy to exploit. In this chapter, we'll dive into how hackers can sniff, clone, and manipulate these systems to cause absolute chaos—from stealing medication to spoofing patient identities. If you thought hospital food was the scariest thing in healthcare, wait until you see what happens when a hacker takes control of the smart hospital system.

The Role of Zigbee and RFID in Smart Hospitals

Before we break into these systems (figuratively, of course), let's understand why hospitals love using Zigbee and RFID:

✓ **Zigbee for Smart Medical Devices** – Used for wireless sensors, smart lighting, temperature monitoring, and even patient-tracking wearables.

✓ **RFID for Asset & Patient Tracking** – Used for scanning medication, tracking medical equipment, and ensuring the right patient gets the right treatment.

✓ **Contactless Authentication** – Doctors and nurses use RFID badges to unlock doors, access medical records, and dispense medication.

Now, imagine if any of these systems got hacked. What happens when an attacker can spoof a nurse's ID badge or reprogram a smart IV pump? Spoiler alert: It's not good.

How Hackers Exploit Zigbee in Smart Hospitals

1. Sniffing and Intercepting Zigbee Traffic

Zigbee devices communicate wirelessly over 2.4 GHz (the same frequency as your Wi-Fi and microwave). If a hacker has a Zigbee sniffer (like a cheap USB dongle), they can eavesdrop on data being transmitted between devices.

📷 **Example Attack**: A hacker sitting in the hospital parking lot captures unencrypted patient data from Zigbee-based health monitors and logs their heart rate, glucose levels, and other sensitive data—all without ever entering the building.

2. Zigbee Network Injection

Zigbee devices form mesh networks, meaning one compromised device can be used to attack others. Attackers can inject fake Zigbee commands to:

✓ **Turn off smart medical sensors** (e.g., disabling temperature monitors in a medicine storage room).

✓ **Manipulate patient data** (e.g., altering readings from glucose monitors).

✓ Create a botnet of infected Zigbee devices to launch further attacks.

📷 **Example Attack**: An attacker injects malicious Zigbee commands that disable all nurse call buttons, making it impossible for patients to request emergency help.

3. Replay Attacks on Zigbee Devices

Since many Zigbee-based hospital systems lack proper encryption, attackers can simply record a legitimate command and replay it later to manipulate devices.

🔊 **Example Attack**: A hacker records a legitimate signal that unlocks the hospital pharmacy and replays it later to gain unauthorized access—walking away with enough painkillers to start a black-market business.

How Hackers Exploit RFID in Hospitals

1. RFID Cloning: Stealing Nurse and Doctor Credentials

RFID is commonly used for hospital ID badges, but many hospitals still use older, unencrypted RFID cards that can be easily cloned.

✓ Attackers use an RFID skimmer to copy a nurse's ID badge.

✓ They create a perfect clone of the badge.

✓ They walk right into restricted hospital areas like they own the place.

🔊 **Example Attack**: A hacker bumps into a doctor in an elevator, secretly scans their badge with a portable RFID reader, and later prints a perfect replica. Now, the hacker has full access to the hospital—without ever hacking a single computer.

2. RFID Spoofing: Manipulating Patient Data

Many hospitals use RFID wristbands for patients, ensuring medications and procedures are given to the right person. But if an attacker spoofs an RFID wristband, they can:

✓ Change a patient's medical records.

✓ Receive treatment meant for someone else.

✓ Cause life-threatening errors in medication dosing.

🔊 **Example Attack**: A hacker clones a cancer patient's RFID wristband, changes the medication dosage instructions, and tricks the system into giving a lethal overdose.

3. Denial-of-Service (DoS) Attacks on RFID Systems

Since RFID readers rely on electromagnetic waves, attackers can use RF jammers to block communication between RFID badges and hospital systems.

✓ Nurses can't access medical supplies.

✓ Doctors can't log into patient records.

✓ Medication dispensing machines stop working.

🔊 **Example Attack**: A hacker disrupts all RFID readers in a hospital wing, locking medical staff out of critical systems and delaying emergency care.

Real-World Zigbee & RFID Attacks in Healthcare

1. RFID Cloning at a Major Hospital

Security researchers demonstrated that hospital RFID badges could be cloned in under 30 seconds using a $50 handheld device. The cloned badge allowed access to operating rooms, patient records, and medication storage.

2. Zigbee Exploits in Smart Hospital Systems

A cybersecurity firm found that many Zigbee-based hospital devices still used default encryption keys, meaning attackers could decrypt and modify medical sensor data in real time.

How to Secure Zigbee and RFID in Smart Hospitals

1. Encrypt Zigbee Communications

✓ Use AES-128 encryption for Zigbee networks.

✓ Ensure devices authenticate commands before execution.

✓ Regularly change encryption keys to prevent replay attacks.

2. Secure RFID Systems

✓ Use encrypted RFID cards instead of easily cloned legacy cards.

✓ Implement multi-factor authentication (MFA) for RFID access.

✓ Deploy RFID detection tools to identify unauthorized skimmers.

3. Prevent Replay Attacks

✓ Implement timestamp-based authentication to prevent replayed commands.

✓ Ensure RFID and Zigbee devices use unique session keys for every transmission.

Final Thoughts: Your Hospital is a Hacker's Playground

Smart hospitals love Zigbee and RFID because they make everything faster and more efficient. But guess what? So do hackers. If a $10 Zigbee sniffer or a cheap RFID cloner can bring an entire hospital's security crashing down, we have a serious problem.

So next time you're in a hospital, take a moment to wonder:

🔒 Is this RFID badge actually secure? Or did some hacker clone it 30 minutes ago? 🔒

Because when it comes to medical IoT security, the scariest exploits aren't just in hacker movies—they're happening right now, in real hospitals, all over the world.

6.5 Defending Against Wireless Threats in Healthcare

If there's one thing hospitals love more than endless paperwork, it's wireless technology. From Wi-Fi-connected patient monitors to Bluetooth insulin pumps, the modern healthcare system is awash in wireless devices. While this makes patient care faster, smarter, and more efficient, it also opens the door to cyberattacks that could put lives at risk.

Imagine a hacker remotely shutting down an infusion pump or jamming the signals of a smart defibrillator. Not great, right? In this chapter, we'll break down the most dangerous wireless threats in healthcare and, more importantly, how to defend against them before someone turns your hospital into a real-life sci-fi horror story.

Understanding Wireless Threats in Healthcare

Wireless networks in hospitals aren't just for doctors checking emails or patients streaming Netflix while waiting for surgery. These networks handle critical patient data, control life-saving devices, and connect everything from infusion pumps to MRI machines.

Key Wireless Technologies in Healthcare:

✓ **Wi-Fi (802.11x)** – Used for hospital-wide networking, remote monitoring, and electronic health record (EHR) systems.

✓ **Bluetooth & BLE (Bluetooth Low Energy)** – Connects wearable medical devices like heart rate monitors and insulin pumps.

✓ **Zigbee & RFID** – Tracks medical assets, patient location, and automates medication dispensing.

✓ **NFC (Near-Field Communication)** – Used for secure access, contactless patient check-ins, and even digital prescriptions.

Each of these wireless technologies brings its own security challenges. From Man-in-the-Middle (MITM) attacks on Wi-Fi to Bluetooth spoofing and RFID cloning, cybercriminals have plenty of ways to wreak havoc in a hospital setting.

The Biggest Wireless Threats in Smart Healthcare

1. Wi-Fi Attacks: Hacking the Hospital's Lifeline

Hospital Wi-Fi networks are often overloaded, outdated, or misconfigured, making them prime targets for hackers.

Common Wi-Fi Threats:

✓ **Rogue Access Points (Evil Twin Attacks):** Hackers set up fake hospital Wi-Fi networks to steal login credentials.

✓ **Packet Sniffing**: Unencrypted patient data can be intercepted using simple tools like Wireshark.

✓ **Wi-Fi Jamming**: Attackers can disrupt critical hospital communications by flooding networks with interference.

🔎 **Real-World Example**: A researcher discovered hospitals using outdated Wi-Fi encryption (WEP!), allowing attackers to crack the network password in minutes and gain access to patient records and IoT medical devices.

2. Bluetooth Exploits: Hijacking Wearable Medical Devices

Bluetooth and BLE (Bluetooth Low Energy) power everything from pacemakers to glucose monitors—but they weren't designed with security first.

Common Bluetooth Threats:

✓ **Bluetooth Sniffing**: Attackers intercept and steal real-time medical data from wearables.

✓ **Device Impersonation**: Hackers mimic legitimate medical devices to inject malicious commands.

✓ **Denial-of-Service (DoS) Attacks**: Flooding a Bluetooth network can shut down all connected devices.

🔘 **Real-World Example**: Security researchers found a critical flaw in a Bluetooth-enabled insulin pump, allowing an attacker to increase or stop insulin delivery remotely—with potentially deadly consequences.

3. RFID & NFC Threats: Stealing Credentials and Patient Data

Hospitals love RFID and NFC for contactless authentication, but hackers love them even more for cloning and eavesdropping on these signals.

Common RFID & NFC Threats:

✓ **Badge Cloning**: Attackers copy hospital ID badges to gain unauthorized access.

✓ **Patient Data Theft**: RFID wristbands can be intercepted and modified to manipulate medical records.

✓ **Replay Attacks**: Hackers record legitimate transactions and replay them to trick hospital systems.

🔘 **Real-World Example**: A security team demonstrated how a stolen RFID badge could be cloned in seconds, allowing them to bypass hospital security and access restricted patient records.

4. Zigbee & IoT Device Attacks: Exploiting Smart Hospital Networks

Hospitals use Zigbee-powered smart sensors to monitor temperature, air quality, and even patient movement—but many devices lack encryption and proper authentication.

Common Zigbee Threats:

✓ **Sniffing Unencrypted Data**: Attackers can intercept sensitive hospital sensor data.

✓ **Command Injection**: Malicious actors send unauthorized commands to manipulate smart hospital devices.

✓ **Botnet Formation**: Compromised Zigbee devices can be recruited into a hospital-wide botnet attack.

🔍 **Real-World Example**: A cybersecurity researcher demonstrated how a Zigbee-based smart lighting system in a hospital could be hacked remotely, shutting down all patient room lights.

Defensive Strategies: Locking Down Wireless Threats in Healthcare

1. Securing Hospital Wi-Fi Networks

✓ **Use WPA3 encryption** – Say goodbye to outdated WEP and WPA2.

✓ **Implement network segmentation** – Keep IoT medical devices on separate VLANs.

✓ **Monitor for rogue access points** – Regularly scan for Evil Twin Wi-Fi attacks.

2. Hardening Bluetooth Medical Devices

✓ **Use strong pairing methods** – Avoid just works mode in favor of authenticated pairing.

✓ **Disable Bluetooth when not in use** – Reduce attack surface.

✓ **Implement Bluetooth whitelisting** – Only allow trusted devices to connect.

3. Strengthening RFID & NFC Security

✓ **Use encrypted RFID badges** – Ditch outdated, cloneable RFID cards.

✓ **Implement multi-factor authentication (MFA)** – Don't rely on RFID alone for security.

✓ **Deploy RFID detection tools** – Identify unauthorized skimmers and cloning attempts.

4. Securing Zigbee and IoT Networks

✓ **Enable encryption on all Zigbee devices** – Prevent data interception.

✓ **Use unique network keys per device** – Avoid default credentials that attackers exploit.

✓ **Monitor for unusual Zigbee activity** – Detect rogue devices attempting to join the network.

Final Thoughts: Wireless Security is Life or Death in Healthcare

The biggest irony in healthcare cybersecurity? The very technology that's saving lives can also be exploited to endanger them. Hospitals are fast adopters of wireless medical tech—but slow adopters of proper security.

If hackers can jam your Bluetooth pacemaker, steal your RFID credentials, and sniff patient records over open Wi-Fi, we have a problem.

So, what's the lesson here? If you work in medical IT security, it's time to take wireless threats seriously. And if you're a patient, maybe ask your doctor if their wireless insulin pump has been penetration tested—because hacking in healthcare isn't a sci-fi movie; it's happening right now. 📟

Chapter 7: Attacking Medical IoT Cloud Services and APIs

Ever wonder how secure your telemedicine app really is? Hint: It's probably not. From weak API authentication to misconfigured cloud storage, attackers don't even need to breach a hospital's internal network when they can just hack the cloud. And when sensitive patient data is sitting on exposed servers, it's basically an all-you-can-steal buffet for cybercriminals.

This chapter examines the security challenges of cloud-connected medical IoT, including API exploitation, remote patient monitoring vulnerabilities, and data leakage risks. We'll explore real-world case studies of cloud-based healthcare breaches and outline best practices for securing medical IoT cloud services to prevent unauthorized access and data exfiltration.

7.1 Understanding Cloud-Connected Healthcare Architectures

Let's be honest—when most people hear the word cloud, they think of two things: "Where did all my photos go?" and "Why is my hospital storing my heart rate data next to cat memes and shopping lists?"

Welcome to cloud-connected healthcare, where life-saving medical devices now talk to massive cloud servers, streaming real-time patient vitals, prescriptions, and diagnostic images to anyone with the right credentials (or, in some cases, the wrong ones). It's a healthcare revolution—but like every revolution, it comes with chaos, vulnerabilities, and hackers rubbing their hands together in anticipation.

So, let's dive in and break down what a cloud-connected healthcare architecture looks like, why it's the future, and most importantly—how to keep cybercriminals from turning your hospital into their personal hacking playground.

What is Cloud-Connected Healthcare?

Cloud-connected healthcare refers to the integration of medical devices, electronic health records (EHRs), telemedicine platforms, and hospital infrastructure with cloud computing services. This architecture allows real-time data access, remote diagnostics, and AI-driven health analytics, improving efficiency, accuracy, and patient outcomes.

Key Components of Cloud-Connected Healthcare:

✓ **Medical IoT Devices** – Sensors, wearables, smart infusion pumps, and implantable medical devices that collect and transmit patient data.

✓ **Edge Computing** – Local processing of critical data before sending it to the cloud, reducing latency and bandwidth usage.

✓ **Cloud Storage & Processing** – Secure cloud platforms like AWS HealthLake, Microsoft Azure for Healthcare, or Google Cloud Healthcare API store and analyze vast amounts of medical data.

✓ **Telemedicine & Remote Monitoring** – Virtual healthcare services allowing doctors to diagnose and treat patients remotely using secure video calls, AI-driven analytics, and remote IoT monitoring.

✓ **EHR & Healthcare Applications** – Electronic health record systems and hospital management applications hosted on the cloud for easy access and collaboration.

🏛 **Real-World Example**: The Mayo Clinic uses cloud-based AI analytics to detect heart disease risks in real time, analyzing thousands of patient ECG readings faster than a human doctor could ever dream of.

How Data Moves in Cloud-Connected Healthcare

Understanding how data moves between patients, devices, and cloud platforms is crucial for securing it. A typical workflow looks like this:

1☐ Patient wears a smart health device (e.g., a glucose monitor).

2☐ The device collects real-time vitals and sends it to a local gateway (smartphone, router, or edge device).

3☐ The data is encrypted and transmitted via Wi-Fi, Bluetooth, or cellular networks to a cloud platform.

4☐ The cloud stores, analyzes, and shares the data with authorized hospital staff, physicians, or AI diagnostic tools.

5️⃣ Healthcare providers access the data through secure dashboards or apps for patient monitoring and treatment.

This sounds amazing, but every step in this process is a potential attack surface. If a hacker intercepts the data mid-transmission or breaches the cloud storage system, your private medical history might not be so private anymore.

Benefits of Cloud-Connected Healthcare (Why Hospitals Love It)

Despite the risks, hospitals can't afford NOT to adopt cloud-connected systems. Why?

✓ **Real-Time Data Access** – Doctors and nurses can instantly retrieve patient records from anywhere, preventing medical errors.

✓ **Cost Efficiency** – Cloud storage eliminates expensive on-site servers, saving hospitals millions in IT costs.

✓ **AI-Driven Diagnostics** – Cloud platforms leverage machine learning to detect diseases early, improving patient outcomes.

✓ **Remote Patient Monitoring** – Chronically ill or elderly patients can be monitored 24/7 without constant hospital visits.

✓ **Disaster Recovery** – Cloud backups ensure that data isn't lost due to cyberattacks, natural disasters, or system failures.

🔘 **Real-World Example**: Cleveland Clinic uses AI-powered cloud analytics to predict heart attack risks before symptoms even appear, helping doctors save lives with proactive care.

The Dark Side: Security Risks in Cloud-Connected Healthcare

Okay, now that we've hyped up the benefits, let's talk about the nightmare scenarios. Cloud-connected healthcare introduces massive cybersecurity risks, including:

1. Data Breaches (Because Hackers Love Medical Records)

Hospitals store valuable personal health information (PHI) in the cloud, making them a prime target for hackers. A single breach can expose millions of patient records, leading to identity theft, insurance fraud, and lawsuits.

Example: In 2023, a major cloud-based healthcare provider suffered a breach, exposing 10 million patient records, including medical histories and insurance details.

2. API Vulnerabilities (The Backdoor to Cloud Data)

Healthcare applications use APIs (Application Programming Interfaces) to send and receive data between devices and cloud servers. If these APIs lack proper authentication and encryption, attackers can bypass security controls and steal sensitive information.

Example: A misconfigured hospital API leaked thousands of patient records when security researchers discovered it was accessible without a password.

3. Ransomware Attacks on Cloud Storage

Ransomware is one of the biggest threats to cloud-based healthcare. Attackers encrypt hospital records and demand a hefty ransom to unlock them. Since lives are on the line, hospitals often pay up, making this attack wildly profitable for cybercriminals.

Example: A ransomware attack forced a hospital to shut down for weeks, delaying surgeries and patient care.

4. Insider Threats & Misconfigurations

Sometimes, the biggest security threat isn't a hacker—it's a careless employee. Misconfigured cloud storage, weak passwords, or disgruntled staff can expose sensitive medical data without even realizing it.

Example: A hospital IT admin left an open database exposed on the internet, leaking 5 million patient records. Oops.

Securing Cloud-Connected Healthcare (How to Fight Back)

The good news? Cloud-connected healthcare doesn't have to be a hacker's playground. Here's how hospitals and security teams can lock it down:

✓ **End-to-End Encryption** – Encrypt all data in transit and at rest to prevent unauthorized access.

✓ **Zero Trust Architecture** – Never assume any user or device is trustworthy; enforce multi-factor authentication (MFA).

✓ **Secure APIs** – Implement strong authentication and rate-limiting to prevent API abuse.

✓ **Cloud Security Posture Management (CSPM)** – Continuously monitor cloud configurations for misconfigurations and vulnerabilities.

✓ **Regular Penetration Testing** – Simulate cyberattacks to identify weak points before attackers do.

✓ **AI-Driven Threat Detection** – Use machine learning algorithms to detect unusual activity in real-time.

Final Thoughts: The Future of Cloud Healthcare Security

Cloud-connected healthcare is revolutionizing medicine, making it faster, more accessible, and smarter than ever before. But with great convenience comes great responsibility—because if we don't secure the cloud, we might as well be handing patient records directly to hackers.

So, what's the takeaway? If you're in healthcare IT, start securing your cloud infrastructure NOW. And if you're a patient, maybe ask your doctor if their telemedicine app has been penetration tested—because your medical secrets deserve better than a leaky cloud server. 🏦

7.2 Exploiting Weak API Authentication in Medical Applications

Let's talk about API security—or, in some cases, the lack of it.

Imagine you walk into a hospital, right past the front desk, straight into the restricted surgical wing—no ID check, no questions, just a polite nod from security. Sounds ridiculous, right? Well, welcome to the wonderfully broken world of weak API authentication, where some medical applications are basically leaving the doors wide open for hackers to stroll in and help themselves to patient records, medical device controls, and even drug prescriptions.

APIs (Application Programming Interfaces) are the backbone of modern healthcare applications, connecting EHR systems, medical IoT devices, telemedicine platforms, and cloud storage. But if these APIs aren't properly secured? Hackers get a free pass to steal, modify, or completely disrupt critical healthcare data.

So, let's dive into how API authentication goes wrong, what attackers can do with these weaknesses, and—most importantly—how to stop them before your pacemaker starts receiving unexpected software updates from a cybercriminal in another country.

The Role of APIs in Healthcare

APIs are the unsung heroes of healthcare IT. They allow systems to communicate and share data, ensuring that doctors, hospitals, and medical devices can exchange critical patient information securely and efficiently.

Common API Use Cases in Healthcare:

✓ **Electronic Health Records (EHRs):** APIs allow hospitals to access and update patient records across different systems.

✓ **Telemedicine Platforms**: APIs enable video consultations, real-time patient monitoring, and online prescription management.

✓ **Medical IoT Devices**: APIs connect smart medical devices—like insulin pumps, heart monitors, and infusion pumps—to cloud dashboards.

✓ **Billing & Insurance Processing**: APIs transmit medical billing details between hospitals, insurers, and payment processors.

When secured properly, APIs streamline healthcare and improve patient outcomes. But when done wrong? They become an open buffet for cybercriminals.

How Weak API Authentication Exposes Medical Data

APIs need authentication to ensure that only authorized users and devices can access medical systems. But unfortunately, some healthcare applications fail at even the most basic security measures. Here's how attackers exploit them:

1. No Authentication (Seriously, None)

Yes, this still happens. Some APIs don't require any authentication at all, allowing anyone with the right URL to pull patient records, device logs, or even system configurations.

🔘 **Example**: Security researchers discovered an exposed medical API that leaked thousands of patient prescriptions—because it didn't even ask for a password.

2. Hardcoded API Keys (A Gift for Hackers)

Developers sometimes hardcode API keys directly into mobile apps or front-end web applications. Once an attacker finds one (which isn't hard), they can access the API as an authenticated user, often with full privileges.

📖 **Example**: A popular telemedicine app accidentally left its API key exposed in its mobile app code, allowing attackers to retrieve private doctor-patient conversations.

3. Weak or Default Credentials (Admin/Admin Strikes Again)

APIs that use default usernames and passwords—or allow weak credentials like password123—are basically begging to be hacked. Attackers simply brute-force or guess their way in.

📖 **Example**: A hospital's patient portal used default API credentials that hadn't been changed since installation. Hackers used them to download 100,000 patient records before anyone noticed.

4. Broken Token Validation (Session Hijacking 101)

APIs often use tokens (like JWT or OAuth tokens) to authenticate users. But if token validation is weak, attackers can:

Reuse stolen tokens to access accounts indefinitely.

Modify token data to escalate privileges.

Trick the system into thinking they're a legitimate doctor, admin, or patient.

📖 **Example**: An EHR system failed to validate API session tokens properly, allowing attackers to impersonate doctors and prescribe medications to fake patients.

5. Lack of Rate Limiting (APIs on Steroids)

APIs without rate limiting allow attackers to brute-force login attempts or enumerate patient records by making thousands of requests per second.

⚖ **Example**: A medical API let attackers cycle through every possible patient ID, retrieving health records one by one—because there was no request limit.

What Can Attackers Do With a Weak API?

When hackers find an exposed medical API, bad things happen fast:

☠ **Steal Patient Data** – Full names, medical histories, test results, prescriptions, insurance details—everything needed for identity theft.

☠ **Modify Medical Records** – Attackers can delete, alter, or inject false data, leading to misdiagnoses and treatment errors.

☠ **Hijack Medical Devices** – APIs controlling infusion pumps, pacemakers, or glucose monitors could be exploited to harm patients directly.

☠ **Inject Ransomware into the System** – Attackers use weak APIs to deploy ransomware, locking hospitals out of critical systems.

☠ **Commit Medical Fraud** – Cybercriminals can bill insurance companies for fake treatments, stealing millions.

Securing Medical APIs: How to Fight Back

The good news? APIs don't have to be an open door for hackers. Here's how to lock them down:

✓ **Require Strong Authentication**: Use OAuth 2.0, API keys, and multi-factor authentication (MFA) for all API requests.

✓ **Enforce Role-Based Access Control (RBAC):** Ensure APIs only grant access to those who need it (e.g., a nurse shouldn't be able to modify billing records).

✓ **Encrypt API Communications**: Use TLS 1.2+ to encrypt data in transit and prevent man-in-the-middle attacks.

✓ **Implement Rate Limiting & Monitoring**: Prevent brute-force attacks by limiting API requests per user/IP.

✓ **Use Secure API Gateways**: API gateways act as shields, filtering traffic, blocking malicious requests, and enforcing security policies.

✓ **Validate Tokens Properly**: Ensure JWTs and OAuth tokens are properly signed, time-limited, and validated on every request.

✓ **Conduct Regular API Penetration Testing**: Simulate attacks to find and fix vulnerabilities before hackers do.

Final Thoughts: Don't Let Your API Be the Weak Link

APIs power the future of healthcare, but without proper security, they're a direct line for hackers to exploit medical data and devices. Hospitals, developers, and security teams must treat API security as a top priority—because one weak API endpoint can be the difference between saving lives and putting them at risk.

So, if you're a healthcare IT professional, pen tester, or developer, start locking down those APIs before someone else does. And if you're a patient? Maybe ask your doctor if their telemedicine app has been penetration tested—because you deserve better than an unsecured API leaking your health records. 🔒

7.3 Hijacking Telemedicine and Remote Patient Monitoring Systems

Let's set the scene. You're sitting on your couch, talking to your doctor over a telemedicine app, discussing your mysterious knee pain that definitely wasn't caused by showing off at basketball practice last weekend. Suddenly, the call freezes. You try to reconnect—no luck. Meanwhile, across the world, a hacker is intercepting your conversation, stealing your medical history, and—oh yeah—possibly injecting malware into the hospital's system.

Sounds like a scene from a cyber-thriller, right? Except it's real. Telemedicine and remote patient monitoring (RPM) systems have revolutionized healthcare, but they've also become prime targets for cybercriminals. From intercepting live consultations to manipulating real-time medical data, attackers can exploit vulnerabilities in these systems with terrifying ease.

So, how do these attacks happen, and what can we do to stop them? Let's dive into the dark side of telemedicine security.

Why Telemedicine & Remote Monitoring Are High-Value Targets

Telemedicine and RPM systems allow patients to consult doctors remotely and continuously track their vitals using connected devices. While convenient, they introduce multiple attack surfaces, including:

✓ **Unsecured Video Calls**: If encrypted improperly, calls can be intercepted.

✓ **Weak API Security**: Attackers can access patient records and control medical devices.

✓ **Compromised IoT Devices**: Hackers can manipulate RPM devices (like insulin pumps and heart monitors).

✓ **Insecure Cloud Storage**: Poor configurations can expose sensitive health data.

For cybercriminals, these systems are goldmines of sensitive data—and sometimes, a gateway to full hospital network access.

How Hackers Hijack Telemedicine & RPM Systems

1. Eavesdropping on Telemedicine Consultations

One of the most common and disturbing attacks is intercepting live doctor-patient calls. Weak encryption, misconfigured servers, or compromised apps can allow hackers to spy on medical conversations, steal medical histories, and even inject false information into the system.

🔎 **Example**: Researchers discovered a major telehealth platform sending unencrypted video streams, allowing attackers to view real-time doctor-patient interactions.

2. Man-in-the-Middle (MITM) Attacks

In MITM attacks, hackers intercept real-time data streams between RPM devices and healthcare providers. This allows them to modify or disrupt patient vitals, potentially leading to incorrect diagnoses or dangerous treatment decisions.

🔎 **Example**: A cybersecurity audit of a remote heart monitor system found that attackers could modify heart rate data, making it look like a patient was in distress—or perfectly fine when they weren't.

3. Exploiting Weak Authentication on RPM Devices

Many remote monitoring devices still use default passwords, making them easy targets for attackers. Once inside, they can tamper with device functionality—or worse, turn devices into zombies for botnet attacks.

🏛 **Example**: A hacker accessed hundreds of insulin pumps by using manufacturer default credentials, potentially allowing remote control over insulin dosages.

4. Ransomware & Medical Data Theft

Telemedicine platforms store vast amounts of patient data. If an attacker breaches one weak API, they can exfiltrate thousands of patient records or inject ransomware into hospital systems, holding critical data hostage.

🏛 **Example**: A ransomware attack on a European telemedicine provider locked out doctors from patient records, delaying treatments for days.

5. Fake Doctor Attacks (Credential Theft & Phishing)

If attackers gain access to doctor accounts, they can impersonate physicians, modify patient prescriptions, or even redirect medical payments.

🏛 **Example**: Hackers used stolen login credentials to prescribe fraudulent medications, leading to fake insurance claims worth millions.

How to Defend Against Telemedicine & RPM Attacks

The good news? These attacks aren't inevitable. Here's how to secure telemedicine and RPM systems:

✓ **End-to-End Encryption (E2EE):** Protects video calls, patient data, and medical streams from interception.

✓ **Multi-Factor Authentication (MFA):** Stops attackers from hijacking doctor or patient accounts.

✓ **Secure API Implementation**: Ensures only authorized users and devices can access patient data.

✓ **Regular Security Patching**: Keeps telemedicine software and RPM devices free from known vulnerabilities.

✓ **Zero-Trust Security Model**: Limits system access based on need-to-know rules.

✓ **Anomaly Detection & AI Monitoring**: Identifies unusual activity—like unexpected device commands or data modifications.

Final Thoughts: Cybersecurity is the New Healthcare Priority

Telemedicine and remote monitoring aren't going anywhere—they're the future of healthcare. But if security isn't a priority, they become a playground for hackers.

As patients, doctors, and security professionals, we need to demand better security from telehealth providers. Stronger encryption, smarter authentication, and proactive monitoring can turn these high-risk systems into truly safe and secure healthcare solutions.

Because let's be real—when you're talking to your doctor about that embarrassing rash, the last thing you want is an anonymous hacker listening in. 🚨

7.4 Data Leakage and Misconfigurations in Healthcare Cloud Storage

Imagine this: A hospital IT admin, in a caffeine-deprived haze, accidentally misconfigures a cloud storage bucket. A few weeks later, patient records—names, diagnoses, insurance details, even MRI scans—are floating around the internet, freely accessible to anyone with a web browser. No hacking skills required. No need for fancy exploits. Just a simple, oops.

Sounds dramatic? Unfortunately, it's one of the most common security failures in healthcare cloud storage today. Misconfigured databases, weak access controls, and exposed backups have led to massive patient data leaks—sometimes affecting millions. And guess what? Hackers love an easy target.

Let's break down why data leaks happen, how cybercriminals exploit them, and what we can do to stop these digital disasters before they happen.

The Danger of Healthcare Cloud Storage Misconfigurations

Healthcare organizations are moving to the cloud at record speed, thanks to the flexibility, scalability, and cost savings. But with great power (read: patient data) comes great responsibility (read: security nightmares).

Here's why misconfigurations and data leaks are such a massive problem:

✓ **Exposed Storage Buckets**: Admins forget to enable authentication, leaving sensitive patient records open to the public.

✓ **Weak Access Controls**: Overly permissive settings let any employee—or even third parties—view sensitive files.

✓ **Unsecured APIs**: Attackers use automated tools to scan for misconfigured APIs and pull patient data at scale.

✓ **Unencrypted Backups**: Even if a system is protected, backups are often stored in plaintext—making them easy pickings for attackers.

✓ **Third-Party Cloud Vendors**: Hospitals rely on external cloud providers who may have poor security practices, exposing data through their missteps.

These mistakes aren't just embarrassing—they lead to regulatory fines, lawsuits, and loss of patient trust.

How Hackers Exploit Healthcare Cloud Leaks

Hackers don't need sophisticated exploits to access misconfigured cloud storage. Most breaches happen because healthcare organizations leave doors wide open.

1. Cloud Bucket Browsing: The "Low-Hanging Fruit" Attack

Many cloud storage services (like AWS S3, Google Cloud Storage, and Azure Blobs) are set to public by default. Cybercriminals use automated tools to scan for publicly accessible storage buckets, revealing millions of unprotected medical records.

🔎 **Example**: In 2020, security researchers found 16 million patient scans (X-rays, MRIs, CT scans) sitting on unprotected cloud storage, freely accessible without authentication.

2. API Exploitation: Stealing Data at Scale

APIs are the backbone of cloud-connected healthcare systems, but poor security practices often leave them wide open. Attackers exploit unauthenticated APIs or use API scraping techniques to extract massive amounts of patient data.

📢 **Example**: A security flaw in a telemedicine provider's API allowed anyone with a patient ID to access medical records, prescription histories, and billing details.

3. Insider Threats & Credential Leaks

Employees—or disgruntled ex-employees—can abuse their access to exfiltrate patient data, either for personal gain or to sell on dark web markets.

📢 **Example**: A hospital IT admin stole 10,000+ patient records and sold them on black market forums for identity theft and insurance fraud.

4. Ransomware Targeting Cloud Backups

Hackers aren't just after patient records—they're also going after cloud-based backups. If backups aren't properly secured or segmented, ransomware attackers can encrypt them too, leaving hospitals completely locked out.

📢 **Example**: The infamous Ryuk ransomware campaign specifically targeted healthcare cloud backups, forcing hospitals to pay millions to regain access.

How to Prevent Data Leaks & Cloud Misconfigurations

The good news? These attacks are preventable. Here's how:

✓ **Lock Down Cloud Storage Buckets**: Set strict access permissions and never leave them public by default.

✓ **Enable Multi-Factor Authentication (MFA):** Protect cloud admin accounts to prevent credential theft.

✓ **Encrypt Data (At Rest & In Transit):** Use strong encryption so even if data is leaked, it remains unreadable.

✓ **Harden APIs with Authentication & Rate Limits**: Require OAuth, API keys, and access controls to prevent unauthorized scraping.

✓ **Implement Zero-Trust Access Policies**: Only allow specific users and systems to access specific cloud resources.

✓ **Regular Security Audits & Penetration Testing**: Simulate attacks to find misconfigurations before hackers do.

✓ **Segment Cloud Backups & Keep Offline Copies**: Ensure backups can't be encrypted by ransomware.

Final Thoughts: The Cloud Can Be Safe—If You Secure It

Cloud storage is a game-changer for healthcare, but let's face it—it's only as secure as the people configuring it. Hospitals, clinics, and telemedicine providers must prioritize cloud security or risk exposing patient data on a global scale.

So next time you hear about a massive healthcare data breach, don't assume it was a nation-state cyberattack. Sometimes, all it takes is a lazy misconfiguration—and a hacker with a search engine. 🔥

7.5 Implementing Secure Cloud Security Measures for MIoT

Let's be honest—when it comes to security, the cloud can be a double-edged scalpel in the world of Medical IoT (MIoT). On one side, it gives us unmatched scalability, remote patient monitoring, and real-time data access. On the other? It's a honeypot of sensitive patient data, just waiting for an attacker to sink their digital claws into.

One misconfiguration, one exposed API, one weak password, and boom—your hospital's cloud storage becomes a buffet for cybercriminals. From ransomware locking up patient records to stolen medical images floating on the dark web, cloud security failures in healthcare aren't just inconvenient—they're life-threatening.

So, how do we lock down cloud environments without breaking the system (or our sanity)? This chapter is your guide to securing MIoT cloud infrastructure—from data encryption and identity management to AI-powered threat detection.

Why Cloud Security Matters in MIoT

Modern healthcare runs on cloud-connected IoT devices. Remote monitoring systems, infusion pumps, wearable ECG trackers, and even robotic surgical tools are all tied to cloud services for data storage, processing, and analytics.

✓ Faster access to patient data from anywhere

✓ Scalability for hospitals, clinics, and telemedicine providers

✓ AI-driven diagnostics and predictive healthcare analytics

✓ Lower infrastructure costs compared to on-premises data centers

But with great connectivity comes even greater security risks. If MIoT devices aren't secured in the cloud, attackers can:

🔒 Hijack medical APIs and extract patient data
🔒 Launch ransomware attacks to hold hospitals hostage
🔒 Exploit misconfigured cloud storage to leak sensitive health records
🔒 Manipulate real-time health monitoring data, leading to false diagnoses

The Core Security Principles for MIoT Cloud Protection

The best defense isn't just patching after a breach—it's building security into the cloud infrastructure from the start. Here are the key pillars of a secure MIoT cloud environment:

1. Zero Trust: Assume Nothing, Verify Everything

- **The old way**: Trust everyone inside the network.
- **The new way**: Trust no one—even internal users and devices.

Zero Trust requires constant verification for every user, device, and application accessing the cloud. Key practices include:

✓ **Least privilege access**: Only give minimum required permissions

✓ **Multi-Factor Authentication (MFA)**: Stop credential-based attacks

✓ **Device health checks**: Restrict access from unpatched or vulnerable devices

2. Strong API Security: The Gateway to Medical Data

APIs are the backbone of cloud-based healthcare—but they're also the #1 target for attackers.

Common API security failures:

✗ **Weak authentication** (e.g., no OAuth, just API keys)
✗ **Poor rate limiting** (attackers can brute-force requests)
✗ **Unencrypted data transfers** (hello, MITM attacks)

How to secure medical APIs:

✓ Use OAuth 2.0 / OpenID Connect for strong authentication

✓ Enable rate limiting to prevent brute-force attacks

✓ Encrypt all API traffic (TLS 1.2 or higher) to protect data in transit

✓ Audit and monitor API access logs for suspicious behavior

3. Encryption: Protecting Patient Data at Every Stage

If there's one rule in cloud security, it's this: Always encrypt sensitive data—at rest, in transit, and even in use.

🚀 **Best encryption practices for MIoT cloud security:**

✓ **Encrypt data at rest**: Use AES-256 encryption for cloud storage

✓ **Encrypt data in transit**: Use TLS 1.2+ to protect data between MIoT devices and the cloud

✓ **Tokenization & anonymization**: Mask sensitive patient data to reduce exposure risks

Bonus tip? Never hardcode encryption keys in source code—use Hardware Security Modules (HSMs) or cloud-native key management solutions.

4. AI & Machine Learning for Cloud Threat Detection

Hackers aren't the only ones using AI—security teams are fighting back with machine learning-powered defenses.

Cloud security providers now offer AI-driven threat detection that:

✓ Monitors cloud traffic for anomalies

✓ Detects suspicious login attempts (e.g., sudden access from Russia at 3 AM?)

✓ Automatically blocks brute-force API attacks

Integrating AI-powered security tools into MIoT cloud infrastructure is no longer optional—it's a requirement.

5. Backup & Disaster Recovery: Always Have a Plan B

Cloud ransomware attacks are skyrocketing, and hospitals are a prime target. The only way to survive? Have a rock-solid backup strategy.

💡 **How to protect cloud backups from ransomware:**

✓ **Use immutable backups** (hackers can't alter them)

✓ **Keep offline backups** (cloud-only backups = ransomware risk)

✓ **Test recovery procedures regularly** (don't wait for an attack to find out your backup doesn't work!)

Future-Proofing MIoT Cloud Security

The cloud is only going to become more critical in healthcare. That means security needs to evolve alongside it.

🔍 **Upcoming trends in MIoT cloud security:**

✓ Confidential computing: Encrypting data even during processing

✓ 5G-enabled MIoT security: Hardening low-latency healthcare networks

✓ Blockchain for medical data integrity: Preventing record tampering

The future of healthcare is in the cloud—but only if we secure it properly.

Final Thoughts: Your Cloud, Your Responsibility

If MIoT cloud security were a horror movie, misconfigurations would be the monster lurking in the shadows—silent, sneaky, and absolutely deadly.

But the good news? You don't have to be the next victim.

By implementing Zero Trust, strong API security, encryption, AI-driven threat detection, and solid backup strategies, we can lock down healthcare cloud environments before attackers get in.

So, before you store one more patient record in the cloud, ask yourself:

☁ Is it secured?
☁ Is it encrypted?
☁ Would I trust it with my own medical history?

If the answer isn't a resounding YES, it's time to fix it—before someone else does. 🔥

Chapter 8: Ransomware, Malware, and Backdoors in Healthcare

Picture this: A hospital is in chaos. Computers are locked. Patients can't get their treatments. And all because some hacker decided to encrypt every system and demand Bitcoin. Ransomware attacks on hospitals aren't just an inconvenience—they're life-threatening. And the worst part? Many of these attacks start with something as simple as an employee clicking a phishing link.

This chapter covers the rise of ransomware and malware targeting healthcare systems, exploring attack methods, case studies (like WannaCry and NotPetya), and strategies for mitigating these threats. We'll also discuss how attackers plant backdoors in medical devices, allowing persistent access even after initial breaches are detected and resolved.

8.1 The Rise of Ransomware in Hospitals and Medical Facilities

If hospitals were movie characters, they'd be that one person who always forgets to lock the front door—only to find a cybercriminal sitting comfortably on their network, encrypting everything in sight. Welcome to the golden age of ransomware in healthcare.

From small clinics to massive hospital networks, ransomware has evolved into one of the most destructive cyber threats in modern medicine. We're not just talking about lost files and downtime; we're talking about life-or-death consequences. Imagine a patient needing immediate surgery, but the hospital's entire system is locked until someone pays a hacker in Bitcoin. That's not just a cybersecurity issue—that's a public health crisis.

So, how did we get here? Why are hospitals such juicy targets? And more importantly, how do we fight back?

How Ransomware Took Over Healthcare

Ransomware didn't start with hospitals—it started as a digital extortion scheme targeting individuals and businesses. The playbook was simple:

Trick users into opening a malicious email attachment or clicking a shady link

Encrypt all their files so they can't access anything

Demand a ransom (usually in cryptocurrency) to restore access

Over time, cybercriminals realized that some organizations simply can't afford downtime—and hospitals quickly rose to the top of that list. Unlike a bank or retail company, hospitals don't have the luxury of "pausing operations" while they deal with an attack.

⚡ Downtime means delayed treatments.
🚑 Delayed treatments mean lives are at risk.
💰 That makes hospitals more likely to pay.

Thus, ransomware gangs shifted their focus to healthcare facilities, where the stakes are high and defenses are often weak.

Why Are Hospitals Prime Targets for Ransomware?

1. Legacy Systems & Outdated Software

Hospitals love old technology—not because they're nostalgic, but because medical devices last longer than their software.

✘ Many hospitals still use Windows 7 (which Microsoft stopped supporting in 2020).

✘ Critical medical devices run on ancient firmware that can't be easily updated.

✘ Custom hospital applications often rely on outdated security models.

When you mix old software with today's ransomware tactics, you get a disaster waiting to happen.

2. Poor Cyber Hygiene Among Staff

Let's face it—doctors and nurses aren't cybersecurity experts. Their priority is saving lives, not spotting phishing emails.

● Clicking suspicious links? Happens all the time.
● Using weak passwords? Yep.
● Sharing login credentials? More common than you'd think.

Hospitals are fast-paced environments where security is often an afterthought, making them an easy entry point for ransomware.

3. Interconnected, High-Stakes Systems

Modern hospitals rely on a network of connected devices—from electronic health records (EHRs) to MRI machines, infusion pumps, and remote monitoring systems.

✓ **More connectivity** = better patient care.

✗ **More connectivity** = more attack surfaces.

A single infected device can spread ransomware across the entire network, shutting down everything from emergency room equipment to billing systems.

4. The "Must-Pay" Factor

Unlike other industries, hospitals can't afford prolonged downtime. If ransomware takes down a manufacturing company, they lose money. If it takes down a hospital, people die.

Cybercriminals exploit this urgency, knowing hospitals are more likely to pay the ransom to get back online ASAP.

Famous Ransomware Attacks in Healthcare

Ransomware has already crippled hospitals worldwide, with some of the most notorious attacks making headlines.

✹ WannaCry (2017) – The Global Outbreak

One of the most infamous ransomware attacks, WannaCry exploited a Windows vulnerability to infect over 300,000 devices worldwide—including dozens of hospitals in the UK's National Health Service (NHS).

🚨 Ambulances were rerouted.

🚨 Surgeries were canceled.

🚨 Medical records were locked.

All because of an unpatched vulnerability.

✸ Ryuk Ransomware – Targeting Hospitals for Profit

Ryuk is one of the deadliest ransomware strains targeting hospitals. Since 2018, it has:

💰 Stolen millions in ransom payments
🚑 Infected entire hospital networks across the U.S.
⚠ Caused massive patient care disruptions

It spreads via phishing emails and unsecured Remote Desktop Protocols (RDPs)—proving that simple security mistakes can cost millions.

✸ Universal Health Services (UHS) Attack (2020)

In one of the largest hospital ransomware attacks, UHS—a major U.S. hospital chain—was hit by Ryuk ransomware.

🚑 Doctors & nurses lost access to electronic health records.
📞 Phone systems went down.
☐ Operations were delayed for days.

The estimated damage? Over $67 million.

How to Defend Against Ransomware in Hospitals

So, how do we fight back against ransomware in hospitals? It all comes down to proactive security measures and better cyber hygiene.

1. Employee Training: Stop Phishing Before It Starts

◆ Teach staff how to recognize phishing emails
◆ Simulate phishing attacks to test awareness
◆ Make cybersecurity training part of hospital culture

2. Stronger Access Controls & Multi-Factor Authentication (MFA)

◆ Use MFA on all critical hospital accounts
◆ Limit access to sensitive data (doctors don't need admin privileges!)

◆ Disable old, unused user accounts (so hackers can't exploit them)

3. Regular Software Updates & Patch Management

◆ Update Windows, Linux, and all medical device software
◆ Disable outdated legacy systems when possible
◆ Apply security patches IMMEDIATELY (especially for known ransomware exploits)

4. Network Segmentation: Contain the Damage

◆ Keep medical IoT devices on separate networks
◆ Isolate critical systems from general hospital networks
◆ Use firewalls & intrusion detection to spot threats early

5. Backup, Backup, Backup (Did We Mention Backup?)

◆ Regularly back up all critical hospital data
◆ Keep backups OFFLINE to prevent ransomware encryption
◆ Test recovery plans frequently (don't wait for an attack to find out your backups don't work!)

Final Thoughts: Ransomware vs. Resilience

Ransomware isn't just another IT issue—it's a direct attack on patient safety.

Hospitals don't have the luxury of hoping attackers won't strike—because they already are. The only way to survive? Prepare, defend, and stay one step ahead.

So, next time you hear about a hospital falling victim to ransomware, ask yourself:

Is my organization next?

If that thought makes you uneasy, it's time to act—before the hackers do. 💀🖥️

8.2 Exploiting Unpatched Medical IoT Devices for Malware Deployment

If hospitals were castles, then medical IoT (MIoT) devices would be the unlocked side doors that no one remembers to check. While IT teams focus on securing servers, firewalls, and EHR systems, hackers are busy sneaking in through infusion pumps, patient monitors, and connected ventilators.

And guess what? Most of these devices run outdated, unpatched software. If a hacker finds one vulnerable device, they can infect it with malware, spread across the hospital's network, and turn critical life-saving equipment into a cybercriminal's playground.

So, why are hospitals filled with unpatched devices? How do attackers exploit them? And more importantly—how do we stop it?

Why Medical IoT Devices Remain Unpatched

Hospitals are notorious for running old, vulnerable technology. It's not because they don't care about security—it's because medical IoT presents unique challenges.

1. Medical Devices Have a Long Lifespan

Unlike consumer electronics, medical devices are built to last 10–15 years (sometimes longer). The problem?

☐ A device from 2010 is still running software from 2010.
☐ Manufacturers rarely provide long-term software updates.
☐ Patching a medical device isn't as easy as updating an app.

And because these devices must meet FDA approval, updating their software can take years—leaving them exposed to modern cyber threats.

2. Fear of Downtime in Hospitals

If a hospital has to choose between patient care and cybersecurity, they'll always pick patient care.

⚠ "We can't shut down the ventilators just to install a patch!"
⚠ "We'll update the MRI software later—right now, we need to scan patients."
⚠ "Rebooting the infusion pumps could put patients at risk!"

Cybercriminals know this hesitation exists, which is why they target unpatched MIoT devices.

3. Lack of Vendor Support for Updates

Some medical device manufacturers don't even offer patches—or, if they do, hospitals have to pay extra for them.

💰 Want a security patch? That's gonna cost you.

☐ Need an update? Wait six months while we get FDA approval.

🔒 Found a vulnerability? Sorry, we don't support that model anymore.

It's a frustrating cycle that keeps hospitals trapped with old, insecure technology.

How Hackers Exploit Unpatched MIoT Devices

Now that we know why medical IoT devices remain unpatched, let's talk about how attackers take advantage of them.

1. Default and Hardcoded Credentials

Most MIoT devices ship with default usernames and passwords, and hospitals rarely change them.

☐ Username: admin | Password: admin
☐ Username: root | Password: 123456
☐ Hardcoded credentials inside firmware

Attackers can easily find these login credentials online and gain access to devices without any hacking skills needed.

2. Remote Code Execution (RCE) Exploits

Unpatched MIoT devices often have flaws that allow hackers to execute malicious code remotely.

Example: A hacker finds a buffer overflow vulnerability in an unpatched MRI scanner. With a simple exploit, they can:

✅ Crash the system (Denial-of-Service attack)

✅ Steal patient scans and medical records

✅ Inject malware that spreads across the hospital network

3. Malware Deployment & Lateral Movement

Once an attacker infects one device, they can spread malware to others.

🚑 Compromise a single infusion pump? Now they have a foothold.
💉 Use that foothold to reach patient monitoring systems.
📡 Hop onto the hospital's Wi-Fi and spread even further.

Before anyone notices, the entire network is compromised.

Real-World MIoT Exploits

☠ WannaCry (2017) – The Ransomware Epidemic

The infamous WannaCry ransomware hit hospitals worldwide, exploiting unpatched Windows devices—including medical equipment running Windows XP.

🚨 300,000+ devices infected
🚨 Hospitals lost access to critical patient data
🚨 Ambulances had to be rerouted

Why did this happen? Because many medical devices were running outdated, unpatched operating systems.

☠ Urgent/11 – The IoT Nightmare

In 2019, researchers discovered 11 critical vulnerabilities in VxWorks, an operating system used in medical devices, patient monitors, and even ventilators.

⚠ These vulnerabilities allowed hackers to take FULL control of devices.
⚠ No authentication needed—just an exploit.
⚠ Many devices remain unpatched to this day.

Defensive Strategies: How to Protect Unpatched MIoT Devices

Okay, we've covered why medical IoT devices are vulnerable and how attackers exploit them—so how do we fight back?

1. Change Default Credentials

First things first: CHANGE THE PASSWORDS.

✕ No more admin:admin logins.

✕ No more root:password.

✓ Use unique, strong passwords for every device.

It's basic security 101, but most hospitals still forget to do this.

2. Implement Network Segmentation

Hospitals should never have MIoT devices on the same network as critical systems.

🔒 Segment MIoT devices onto isolated networks.
🔒 Use VLANs to separate patient data from IoT traffic.
🔒 Deploy firewalls and intrusion detection systems (IDS).

If a hacker infects one device, network segmentation prevents them from spreading.

3. Apply Virtual Patching (If Regular Patching Isn't an Option)

If a device can't be patched, use virtual patching—a technique where:

✓ Network-based security solutions block known exploits

✓ Firewalls filter out malicious traffic

✓ Endpoint protection detects and stops suspicious behavior

It's not as good as a real patch, but it's better than nothing.

4. Monitor and Log MIoT Activity

Hospitals should track all medical IoT device activity in real time.

👀 Log every connection attempt.

🔍 Set up alerts for unusual activity.

🚨 Automatically block suspicious traffic.

Many MIoT attacks go unnoticed for weeks because no one is monitoring these devices.

Final Thoughts: The Unpatched Epidemic

Hospitals are supposed to save lives, not become playgrounds for cybercriminals. Yet, as long as unpatched MIoT devices remain connected to critical hospital networks, hackers will continue exploiting them with ease.

So, what's the solution?

💉 Treat cybersecurity like patient safety.

☐ Patch and secure devices just like you maintain medical equipment.

🔒 Lock down IoT networks BEFORE attackers exploit them.

Because if we don't? The next ransomware outbreak could be just one unpatched device away. 🚑💀

8.3 Creating and Injecting Backdoors in Connected Medical Systems

If medical IoT devices were medieval castles, backdoors would be the secret tunnels leading straight past the guards, through the kitchen, and into the throne room. And guess what? Hackers love secret tunnels.

Why? Because once they plant a backdoor inside a connected medical system, they can sneak in whenever they want, stay hidden, and do whatever they please—steal data, manipulate devices, or even launch ransomware attacks.

Backdoors in medical IoT (MIoT) are a nightmare for cybersecurity teams. Once an attacker gains persistent access, kicking them out becomes nearly impossible. So, let's talk about how backdoors are created, how they get injected into medical devices, and most importantly—how we can stop them.

What Exactly Is a Backdoor?

A backdoor is an intentional or unintentional way for attackers to bypass security measures and gain access to a system without proper authentication.

Some backdoors are left behind by developers for troubleshooting. Others are created by hackers who infiltrate a system and want to maintain long-term access. Either way, once a backdoor exists, it's an open invitation for exploitation.

How Backdoors Are Created in Medical Systems

1. Hardcoded Credentials in Firmware

Oh look, another device with "admin:password" buried inside the firmware.

Some medical devices ship with hardcoded usernames and passwords that can't be changed. These backdoors exist because:

◆ Manufacturers use default logins for maintenance and forget to remove them.
◆ Hospitals don't update credentials because they don't even know they exist.
◆ Attackers reverse-engineer the firmware, find these credentials, and log in effortlessly.

Once a hacker finds hardcoded credentials, they can log in remotely and create their own hidden access points.

2. Exploiting Remote Access Tools

Many medical devices support remote access for technicians to perform diagnostics and updates.

⚠ But what happens if an attacker gains access to those tools?

They can:

✓ Create new admin accounts that bypass normal authentication.

✓ Modify system settings to disable security features.

✓ Install additional malware that ensures they always have a way back in.

3. Modifying Medical Device Firmware

Hackers with physical or remote access to a device can inject backdoors directly into its firmware.

🔩 **Example**: A cybercriminal reverses the firmware of a pacemaker programmer and plants malicious code that lets them remotely control implanted devices.

Once the infected firmware is installed:

◆ The attacker now has persistent access.
◆ Even factory resets won't remove the backdoor.
◆ Updates won't help—unless the vulnerability itself is patched.

4. Compromising APIs in Connected Healthcare Systems

Modern hospitals heavily rely on APIs to exchange patient data, control medical IoT devices, and manage healthcare applications.

If an attacker finds an insecure API, they can:

◆ Exploit weak authentication to gain unauthorized access.
◆ Inject malicious code that creates hidden admin accounts.
◆ Modify API requests to install malware onto connected devices.

Once an attacker injects a backdoor via an API, they can access medical systems anytime, even if the original vulnerability is patched.

Real-World Medical IoT Backdoor Exploits

💀 Backdoor in CT Scanners

Security researchers discovered that many CT scanners had hidden manufacturer accounts, allowing remote logins with default credentials.

◆ **Problem**: Hospitals had no idea these accounts existed.
◆ **Consequence**: Attackers could remotely access and control scanning machines.
◆ **Impact**: Unauthorized changes to radiation settings could have deadly consequences.

☠ Hidden Backdoors in Patient Monitors

In 2022, researchers found hardcoded SSH credentials inside hospital patient monitoring systems.

⚠ Attackers who accessed these systems could:

✅ Modify patient vital signs in real time.

✅ Disable alarms that alert doctors to critical conditions.

✅ Exfiltrate sensitive patient data.

These backdoors were not officially documented—even the hospitals using the devices had no idea they existed.

How to Defend Against Medical IoT Backdoors

1. Conduct Regular Penetration Testing

Hospitals should regularly test their medical IoT devices for hidden backdoors.

🔍 Hire ethical hackers to perform firmware analysis and source code audits.
🔍 Scan for hardcoded credentials in devices before deployment.
🔍 Test APIs for authentication flaws that could be exploited.

If backdoors are found, work with manufacturers to patch them ASAP.

2. Disable Unnecessary Remote Access

Most backdoors rely on remote access tools to stay open.

✔ Disable remote access unless absolutely necessary.

✔ Use multi-factor authentication (MFA) for all admin logins.

✔ Monitor remote access logs for suspicious activity.

If a device doesn't need to be accessed from outside the hospital network, BLOCK IT.

3. Encrypt API Communications and Secure Authentication

If your APIs don't have strong authentication, attackers will find ways to inject backdoors.

🔒 Use API keys and OAuth for authentication.
🔒 Encrypt API traffic using TLS 1.2 or higher.
🔒 Limit API access to trusted devices only.

Securing APIs ensures attackers can't exploit weak endpoints to inject malware.

4. Keep Firmware Updated (And Verify Patches)

Updating firmware isn't enough—you need to verify that updates remove vulnerabilities.

✓ Check manufacturer changelogs to confirm security patches.

✓ Scan updated firmware for hidden backdoors.

✓ Block outdated firmware versions from running on hospital networks.

If a device can't be patched, hospitals should consider replacing it or isolating it on a segmented network.

5. Implement Continuous Monitoring and Threat Detection

Hospitals need real-time security monitoring for medical IoT devices.

👀 Log all login attempts and remote access events.
🚨 Set up alerts for unauthorized firmware modifications.
☐ Use intrusion detection systems (IDS) to catch suspicious activity.

If a backdoor is being used, you need to detect and shut it down immediately.

Final Thoughts: Closing the Secret Tunnels

Backdoors in medical IoT are not just theoretical threats—they are real, dangerous, and actively exploited.

🩹 Think of cybersecurity like patient care. You wouldn't ignore an infection until it spreads, so don't ignore security vulnerabilities until they become breaches.

If hospitals and device manufacturers don't take medical IoT security seriously, attackers will continue using backdoors to compromise patient safety, steal data, and hold hospitals hostage.

So, what's the solution?

🚑 Patch your devices.
⬜⬜ Harden remote access.
🔍 Monitor for hidden backdoors before attackers find them.

Because in a world where hackers can manipulate life-saving devices, the only way to keep patients safe is by locking every secret tunnel before it's too late. 🔒

8.4 Case Studies: NotPetya, WannaCry, and Medical Ransomware Attacks

If hospitals were action movies, ransomware attacks would be the part where the villain locks down the entire city, demands a ransom, and laughs maniacally while the heroes scramble to fix things.

Except this isn't a movie. It's real life. And the consequences are far worse than just dramatic explosions.

When ransomware hits a hospital, it's not just about money—it's about patients, lives, and critical care being held hostage. A locked medical system means ventilators stop working, pacemakers go offline, patient records disappear, and surgeries are delayed.

In this chapter, we'll dive into some of the most infamous ransomware attacks that crippled the healthcare sector—NotPetya, WannaCry, and other major medical ransomware incidents. Buckle up; this is going to be a wild ride.

The Notorious NotPetya Attack (2017): A Hospital's Worst Nightmare

What Happened?

June 27, 2017. A seemingly innocent software update turned into a global cyber catastrophe.

NotPetya was a weaponized piece of ransomware disguised as a tax software update. It spread like wildfire, locking down networks, encrypting files, and destroying data across industries—including healthcare.

One of the biggest victims? The National Health Service (NHS) in the UK.

How NotPetya Wreaked Havoc on Healthcare

Once NotPetya infiltrated a system, it did two terrifying things:

✓ It spread laterally across hospital networks without user interaction.

✓ It permanently destroyed data—even if the ransom was paid.

This meant hospitals couldn't just "restore" their systems. It was total annihilation.

Impact on hospitals:

Over 1,200 NHS systems were crippled—from patient records to MRI machines.

Ambulances had to be rerouted because hospitals couldn't access patient data.

Surgeries were canceled because operating room computers were bricked.

Critical care patients were transferred as hospitals scrambled to regain control.

NotPetya wasn't even about money. It was destruction disguised as ransomware. The ransom message was fake—there was no way to recover encrypted files.

Cost to the healthcare sector? Over $10 billion in damages.

The WannaCry Outbreak (2017): The Digital Pandemic

What Happened?

May 12, 2017—WannaCry shut down hospitals around the world.

WannaCry was a self-spreading ransomware worm that exploited a Microsoft Windows vulnerability called EternalBlue.

It didn't just lock files—it spread across networks without any human interaction. One infected computer could cripple an entire hospital in minutes.

How WannaCry Crushed Hospitals

The biggest victim? The UK's NHS (again).

Within hours, WannaCry infected over 300,000 devices in 150 countries.

🚑 Hospitals were forced to turn away patients.
💉 Medical devices, including MRI scanners, were rendered useless.
💼 Patient records became inaccessible, delaying treatments.
☐ Some hospitals had to revert to pen-and-paper operations.

How did it spread so fast?

Unpatched Windows systems were vulnerable to EternalBlue.

No user action was needed. WannaCry spread on its own.

Hospitals were using outdated software—some running Windows XP (yes, from 2001!).

The worst part? A security patch for the vulnerability existed TWO MONTHS before the attack. But because many hospitals hadn't updated their systems, they were left defenseless.

The damage? WannaCry cost the NHS $92 million and caused massive patient care disruptions.

Other Medical Ransomware Attacks That Shook the Industry

💀 The Ryuk Ransomware Attack (2019–2020)

Ryuk ransomware targeted over 250 hospitals across the U.S., encrypting systems and demanding millions in ransom.

🚑 Ambulances were diverted as ER systems went offline.
💰 Some hospitals paid the ransom just to regain access to patient records.
📅 Scheduled treatments—including cancer care—were delayed.

Ryuk spread through phishing emails—a simple click on a bad link, and hospitals were locked down.

💀 The Conti Ransomware Attack (2021)

Conti ransomware hit Ireland's entire healthcare system, paralyzing hospitals for weeks.

70% of medical IT systems were taken offline.

Doctors lost access to patient history and medical imaging.

COVID-19 treatments were delayed due to system failures.

The attackers demanded $20 million in ransom, but the Irish government refused to pay. Recovery took months.

Why Are Hospitals a Prime Target for Ransomware?

1⎵ They rely on outdated software.

Many hospitals still use Windows XP or other unpatched systems, making them easy targets.

2⎵ Medical devices aren't built with security in mind.

MRI machines, infusion pumps, and patient monitors were designed for function, not security.

3⎵ Hospitals can't afford downtime.

A locked system means patient care stops, forcing hospitals to pay the ransom quickly.

4⎵ Healthcare data is extremely valuable.

Stolen patient records sell for $250+ per record on the dark web.

How to Defend Against Medical Ransomware

1. Patch Everything—Yesterday

If hospitals had patched Windows before WannaCry, the attack wouldn't have happened.

✓ Apply security patches as soon as they're released.

✓ Upgrade outdated operating systems (RIP Windows XP).

2. Isolate Medical Devices from Hospital Networks

Most MRI scanners and infusion pumps don't need direct internet access.

✓ Segment medical IoT devices into separate networks.

✓ Use firewalls to block unnecessary connections.

3. Back Up Everything (And Test the Backups!)

Backups won't help if they're also encrypted by ransomware.

✓ Keep offline backups that ransomware can't touch.

✓ Regularly test backups to ensure they can be restored.

4. Implement Multi-Factor Authentication (MFA)

Ransomware gangs often use stolen credentials to break in.

✓ Enforce MFA on all hospital admin accounts.

✓ Limit privileged access to critical systems.

Final Thoughts: The Fight Against Ransomware Continues

Ransomware isn't going away. If anything, it's getting worse.

Healthcare will always be a top target because lives depend on technology. That's why it's critical for hospitals to start treating cybersecurity as seriously as patient care.

🩹 **Think of security patches like vaccines**—if you skip them, you're vulnerable to an outbreak.

🚑 **Regular penetration testing is like a check-up**—catch problems before they get worse.

🔒 **A strong cybersecurity strategy is like a well-trained ER team**—it needs to be fast, proactive, and ready for anything.

The bottom line? Cybercriminals don't care about patient lives. But we do.

And that means we fight back, harden our defenses, and never let ransomware win. 🚀

8.5 Strategies to Mitigate Ransomware and Malware in Smart Healthcare

If ransomware had a personality, it would be that annoying guest who crashes your party, eats all the food, trashes the place, and then demands money before they leave. But unlike an annoying guest, ransomware doesn't just disappear—it shuts down hospitals, locks patient records, and puts lives at risk.

Hospitals and healthcare facilities have become prime targets for ransomware gangs because they can't afford downtime—which makes them more likely to pay up. But handing over millions to cybercriminals isn't exactly a sustainable business model (or a good look for patient care).

So, how do we fight back? How do we make hospitals ransomware-proof? Let's break down real-world, effective strategies that actually work.

1. Patch Everything, Everywhere, All at Once

Look, I get it—patching sucks. Nobody likes downtime, and medical systems aren't exactly easy to update. Some hospitals still run Windows XP (which should be a crime, honestly). But here's the thing:

💀 WannaCry wouldn't have happened if hospitals had patched.

💀 NotPetya wouldn't have spread if systems were up to date.

◆ Apply critical security patches ASAP.

- Upgrade outdated operating systems (yes, that means finally ditching Windows XP).
- Use automated patch management tools to avoid human error.

Skipping patches is like refusing a vaccine—it only takes one unpatched system to infect an entire network.

2. Network Segmentation: Keep the Bad Guys Contained

Think of network segmentation like a hospital floor plan—you wouldn't let random visitors wander into the ICU or the OR, right? The same logic applies to cybersecurity.

- Separate critical medical IoT devices from regular IT networks.
- Use VLANs (Virtual LANs) to create isolated security zones.
- Block unnecessary communication between devices.

So if one system gets hit with ransomware, it stays contained—instead of turning into a hospital-wide meltdown.

3. Implement Strong Access Controls (Because Not Everyone Needs Admin Privileges)

If an attacker gets admin access, it's game over.

- 💀 No MFA? Hackers will love you.
- 💀 Shared passwords? Might as well gift-wrap the keys to your network.
- 💀 Default credentials? Congrats, you just made a hacker's day.

- Enforce Multi-Factor Authentication (MFA) on all accounts.
- Use the principle of least privilege (only give access to what's necessary).
- Regularly audit user permissions and remove inactive accounts.

4. Backups: Your Cybersecurity Safety Net

Ransomware works because victims don't have backups—or worse, their backups get encrypted too.

- **Use the 3-2-1 backup strategy:**

✓ 3 copies of your data

✓ 2 different storage mediums

✓ 1 offsite, air-gapped backup

◆ Test your backups regularly. A backup that doesn't work is just as useless as no backup.

◆ Store backups offline. If ransomware can't reach it, it can't encrypt it.

When hospitals have secure, tested backups, they can recover without paying a ransom.

5. Email Security: Because Phishing is STILL a Problem

Most ransomware infections start with one bad email. One employee clicks a malicious link, and BOOM—entire hospital down.

◆ Train employees to recognize phishing emails. (Yes, that includes doctors, nurses, and admins.)
◆ Use email filtering to block suspicious attachments and links.
◆ Deploy DMARC, DKIM, and SPF records to prevent email spoofing.

If phishing is the front door to ransomware, good email security keeps that door locked.

6. Endpoint Detection and Response (EDR): Your Cybersecurity Watchdog

Traditional antivirus isn't enough anymore. Ransomware evolves too fast.

EDR solutions continuously monitor endpoints for suspicious activity—so even if ransomware gets in, it gets caught before it spreads.

◆ Deploy EDR on all hospital workstations and servers.
◆ Use AI-driven threat detection to catch anomalies in real time.
◆ Automate response actions to stop ransomware before it locks systems.

Think of EDR as your hospital's cybersecurity ER team—ready to react instantly.

7. Zero Trust Security: Because Trusting Everything is a Bad Idea

Zero Trust = Assume Nothing is Safe.

Hospitals have too many attack surfaces—from medical IoT devices to remote workstations. Zero Trust forces everything to prove it's legitimate.

- ◆ Enforce strict authentication for ALL network connections.
- ◆ Verify every access request (even from "trusted" users).
- ◆ Micro-segment networks to limit lateral movement.

If ransomware can't move freely, it can't take down an entire hospital.

8. Incident Response: Have a Plan BEFORE Disaster Strikes

When a hospital gets hit with ransomware, every second counts. Without a plan, panic takes over.

- ◆ Develop a ransomware incident response plan.
- ◆ Run tabletop exercises to simulate attacks.
- ◆ Have a dedicated response team that knows EXACTLY what to do.

If an attack happens, contain, isolate, and recover—without making panic-driven mistakes.

9. Don't Pay the Ransom (Unless It's Life or Death)

Look, I get it—when lives are on the line, paying the ransom seems like the fastest way out. But here's the harsh truth:

💀 Paying doesn't guarantee file recovery.
💀 It funds more cybercrime.
💀 It makes hospitals a bigger target for future attacks.

If a hospital has solid backups, it can recover without paying. If it doesn't, it's at the mercy of cybercriminals.

Final Thoughts: Fighting Back Against Ransomware in Healthcare

Ransomware in hospitals isn't just an IT problem—it's a patient safety issue. If systems go down, people die.

But the good news? We CAN fight back.

🪥 **Patching is like getting vaccinated**—do it before an outbreak happens.
🚑 **Network segmentation is like triage**—keep infections from spreading.
🔒 **Zero Trust is like a security checkpoint**—don't let threats roam freely.

The bottom line? Cybercriminals are getting smarter, but so can we. The more we harden our defenses, the less power ransomware has.

Hospitals are meant for saving lives, not paying ransoms. Let's keep it that way. 🚀

Chapter 9: Physical Security and Side-Channel Attacks

What if I told you a hacker could steal data from a pacemaker just by standing near you? Or that medical devices could be compromised physically without ever connecting to a network? From extracting encryption keys to tampering with hardware, physical and side-channel attacks on medical IoT are a whole new level of scary.

In this chapter, we explore threats that involve direct physical access to medical IoT devices, including hardware manipulation, side-channel attacks, and reverse engineering medical implants. We'll also discuss countermeasures to protect these devices from unauthorized physical access and tampering.

9.1 Physical Access Exploits on Smart Medical Devices

Imagine you walk into a hospital room, and instead of a clipboard hanging on the bed, there's a beeping, blinking smart infusion pump. Across the room, a nurse checks a tablet-controlled ventilator, while a doctor adjusts a wirelessly connected pacemaker from a mobile app.

Welcome to modern healthcare—where everything is "smart," networked, and hackable.

Now, what if I told you that half the security concerns we stress about (firewalls, encryption, authentication) don't matter if an attacker can just walk in and plug into the device? Yep. Physical access = game over.

Hospitals are public spaces. Unlike a corporate office with security badges, anyone can walk into a hospital—visitors, vendors, or that one guy who insists he needs to check on his imaginary pet goldfish in the ICU. And if someone with bad intentions gets their hands on a medical device, they can hack it, manipulate it, or even weaponize it.

Let's break down how attackers exploit physical access to medical devices—and how we can stop them.

1. The Danger of Unattended, Unsecured Medical Devices

Most hospitals have hundreds, if not thousands, of smart medical devices—from patient monitors to drug infusion pumps, all running custom firmware. Many of these devices have:

- USB ports that allow data access or firmware updates
- Debugging interfaces that developers forgot to lock down
- Serial ports that provide direct control over the device
- Default login credentials that manufacturers never expected users to change

All of this makes physical security a nightmare. A hacker doesn't need an internet connection if they can just plug in a cable and take control.

💻 **Example Attack**: A researcher demonstrated how simply inserting a USB drive into a hospital's medical workstation allowed malware to spread across the network—infecting X-ray machines, patient record systems, and even ventilators.

2. USB Attacks: The Trojan Horse of Healthcare

Hospitals are notorious for having open USB ports everywhere—on workstations, medical imaging devices, and patient monitors. And hackers? They love USB ports.

- **BadUSB Attacks**: A malicious USB device looks like a normal flash drive but can execute hidden scripts, inject malware, or even impersonate a keyboard to type out malicious commands.
- **Rubber Ducky Attacks**: A tiny USB device automates keystrokes—stealing credentials, disabling security settings, or creating backdoors.
- **USB Killers**: Some USB devices can send high-voltage surges, frying the electronics inside critical medical devices.

💻 **Example Attack**: A cybersecurity researcher once left a few USB drives in a hospital waiting room labeled "Patient Records – Confidential". Within hours, multiple employees plugged them into workstations out of curiosity, giving the simulated attacker complete system access.

🔒 **Defense Strategy:**

✅ Disable USB ports on all medical IoT devices unless absolutely necessary.

✅ Use USB whitelisting software to allow only trusted devices.

☑ Train hospital staff to NEVER plug in unknown USB drives (curiosity is dangerous).

3. Direct Console and Debug Port Access

Many medical devices have debug ports (such as UART, JTAG, or Serial Interfaces) that allow technicians to troubleshoot or update firmware. These ports are often left wide open with no authentication.

For a hacker, this is like finding a secret backdoor to the device's brain. With a simple cable and a laptop, they can:

◆ Dump the firmware and analyze it for vulnerabilities.

◆ Bypass authentication and gain root access.

◆ Modify device behavior—like changing how a pacemaker delivers shocks or how an insulin pump dispenses medication.

🏮 **Example Attack**: Security researchers hacked a hospital's infusion pumps by accessing an unprotected serial port, allowing them to change medication dosages remotely.

🔒 **Defense Strategy:**

☑ Physically block access to debug ports using epoxy or security covers.

☑ Disable debugging interfaces in production devices.

☑ Use tamper-evident seals to detect unauthorized access.

4. The Danger of Stolen or Cloned Access Cards

Hospitals use RFID keycards to restrict access to sensitive areas. But guess what? Most RFID systems are easily cloned.

◆ **RFID Cloning**: A hacker with a cheap RFID reader ($50 on eBay) can walk past a nurse, scan their badge, and copy it to a blank card in seconds.

◆ **Relay Attacks**: Attackers can use a device to extend the range of a keycard—tricking hospital doors into unlocking remotely.

◆ **Stolen Access Cards**: Many hospital staff leave badges unattended at nursing stations. If an attacker picks one up, they can walk right into restricted areas.

🔔 **Example Attack**: A penetration tester entered a hospital, sat in the waiting area, and discreetly scanned dozens of RFID badges. Later, he cloned them and walked into the restricted server room like he belonged there.

🔒 **Defense Strategy:**

✓ Use encrypted RFID cards (not cheap, easily cloned ones).

✓ Implement biometric access in critical areas (fingerprint or retina scan).

✓ Train staff to report lost or stolen access cards immediately.

5. Evil Maid Attacks: When an Attacker Has Time Alone with a Device

The "Evil Maid" attack is named after the idea that a malicious cleaner in a hotel room could tamper with a laptop left unattended. The same thing applies to medical devices in hospitals.

If an attacker gains access to an unattended MRI machine, infusion pump, or even a workstation, they can:

- Install malware or keyloggers.
- Tamper with hardware (implanting malicious chips).
- Steal patient data by extracting hard drives.

🔔 **Example Attack**: In 2018, researchers implanted a small Wi-Fi chip into a medical device that allowed them to remotely access it from miles away.

🔒 **Defense Strategy:**

✓ Physically lock down devices when not in use.

✓ Use tamper-proof screws and locks on device casings.

✓ Install intrusion detection systems to alert when devices are opened.

Final Thoughts: Physical Security is Cybersecurity

We spend so much time worrying about firewall rules, encryption, and network security that we forget the most basic security rule:

🔊 If an attacker can touch it, they can own it. 🔊

Hospitals are high-risk environments, and securing physical access to medical IoT devices is just as important as securing the network.

So next time you see an unlocked medical workstation, an open USB port, or a nurse's RFID badge left on a desk, just remember—that's all a hacker needs to take control.

🔒 Lock it down. Secure it. And stop making life easy for attackers. 💉

9.2 Extracting Data from Wearable Health Devices

Wearables: The Fitness Frenzy That Became a Hacker's Playground
Once upon a time, we wore watches that just told time. Simple days, right? Now, we have smartwatches tracking our heartbeats, glucose levels, sleep cycles, and even stress levels. We've essentially turned into walking, breathing, Wi-Fi-connected data streams.

From Fitbits to smart ECG monitors, continuous glucose monitors (CGMs), and even AI-powered hearing aids, wearable health devices have revolutionized personal healthcare. But they've also introduced a security nightmare—one that hackers are thrilled about.

Because here's the kicker: Most wearable health devices prioritize user convenience over security. Why? Well, imagine if your smartwatch made you type in a 16-character password every time you wanted to check your steps—people would riot. So, security takes a back seat, and that's exactly where attackers find their opportunity.

In this section, we're diving into how hackers extract data from wearable health devices, why it's a massive privacy risk, and what we can do to stop it.

1. How Wearables Store and Transmit Data

Wearable health devices are tiny but mighty. They collect an insane amount of data, including:

◆ **Heart rate & ECG readings** – Monitored by fitness trackers and medical-grade wearables.

◆ **Glucose levels** – Critical data for diabetic patients using CGMs.

◆ **Sleep patterns** – Because, of course, your smartwatch needs to know how often you toss and turn.

◆ **GPS location data** – For runners, cyclists, and anyone who forgot to turn off location tracking.

◆ **Activity logs & movement tracking** – Good for fitness… and good for stalkers.

This data is often stored locally on the device, transferred to a mobile app via Bluetooth, and then synced to the cloud. Each of these steps is a potential attack point.

📟 **Example Attack**: A researcher found that certain wearables store raw health data in unencrypted local storage, meaning anyone with physical access could extract it without needing credentials.

2. Bluetooth Sniffing: Eavesdropping on Wearable Devices

Most wearables use Bluetooth Low Energy (BLE) to sync with smartphones. BLE is great for saving battery life but horrible for security when improperly implemented.

◆ Unencrypted Bluetooth traffic can be intercepted using tools like Ubertooth One or a simple Raspberry Pi with a Bluetooth dongle.

◆ Pairing vulnerabilities in older wearables allow attackers to spoof a connection and extract data.

◆ Man-in-the-middle (MITM) attacks can let hackers intercept and modify health data before it reaches the cloud.

📟 **Example Attack**: A security researcher demonstrated how a fake Bluetooth device could trick certain smartwatches into syncing with it instead of the user's phone—allowing complete access to health data.

🔒 **Defense Strategy:**

✓ Use encrypted Bluetooth communication (AES-128 or higher).

✓ Disable automatic pairing and require manual confirmation for new connections.

✓ Monitor Bluetooth connections and alert users of unknown devices.

3. Extracting Data from Wearable Companion Apps

Wearables rely on mobile apps to display data, set up device settings, and sync with cloud services. Unfortunately, poorly secured apps are a hacker's goldmine.

◆ **Reverse Engineering Apps** – Attackers decompile wearable apps to find API keys, hardcoded credentials, and hidden developer features.

◆ **Weak API Authentication** – Many wearables use insecure API endpoints, allowing attackers to pull data without proper credentials.

◆ **Session Hijacking** – If the app stores authentication tokens insecurely, an attacker can steal login credentials and take over accounts.

🔎 **Example Attack**: A security researcher found that a major fitness tracker's API didn't require authentication for some requests—meaning anyone could pull health data just by guessing a user ID.

🔒 **Defense Strategy:**

✅ Secure API endpoints with proper authentication and rate limiting.

✅ Encrypt stored authentication tokens and use biometric authentication for app logins.

✅ Perform regular security audits on wearable companion apps.

4. Cloud-Based Wearable Data Breaches

Since wearables sync to the cloud, a breach of the cloud service means every user's health data is exposed.

◆ Misconfigured cloud storage (hello, open AWS buckets!) can leak sensitive health records.

◆ Weak passwords on wearable accounts allow hackers to log in and steal data.

◆ Phishing attacks trick users into giving up credentials, giving attackers full access.

🔎 **Example Attack**: In 2018, a fitness tracking company accidentally exposed military base locations because soldiers wore GPS-enabled fitness trackers that uploaded running routes to a publicly accessible cloud map.

🔒 Defense Strategy:

✅ Use strong encryption (end-to-end) for cloud-stored health data.

✅ Implement multi-factor authentication (MFA) for wearable accounts.

✅ Regularly audit cloud storage for misconfigurations.

5. Physical Access Attacks: Dumping Data Directly from Wearables

If a hacker can get their hands on a wearable device, it's game over. Many wearables store data in unencrypted memory, meaning an attacker can extract it just by connecting the device to a computer.

◆ **Memory Dumping** – Attackers extract raw storage and recover logs, passwords, and health data.

◆ **Debugging Interfaces** – Some wearables have hidden debug ports (JTAG, UART) that give full system access.

◆ **Firmware Extraction & Modification** – By dumping firmware, hackers can modify a wearable's behavior or inject malicious code.

🔍 **Example Attack**: A hacker extracted a full activity log from a stolen smartwatch, revealing GPS locations and private medical data.

🔒 Defense Strategy:

✅ Encrypt stored data with strong encryption (AES-256).

✅ Disable unused debug ports and interfaces.

✅ Use secure boot mechanisms to prevent firmware tampering.

Final Thoughts: Wearables Are Fun… Until They Aren't

Wearable health devices are amazing innovations, but they also pose serious security risks. From Bluetooth vulnerabilities to cloud breaches and physical attacks, hackers have way too many ways to extract data from wearables.

So, the next time you strap on your fancy smartwatch, just remember—it's not just tracking your steps… it might be tracking you, too. 👀🔓

🔒 Stay secure, encrypt everything, and maybe—just maybe—turn off that GPS tracking once in a while. ☺

9.3 Side-Channel Attacks on Implantable Medical Devices (IMDs)

Welcome to the Cyberpunk Reality of Hacked Heartbeats

Once upon a time, the scariest thing about a pacemaker was the hospital bill. Fast forward to today, and hackers can potentially weaponize implantable medical devices (IMDs). It sounds like a scene out of a sci-fi thriller—except it's very real.

Imagine a world where a cybercriminal could remotely reprogram a pacemaker, disrupt an insulin pump's dosage, or drain the battery of a life-saving neurostimulator. The craziest part? They wouldn't even need direct access to the device—they could do it just by analyzing signals and power consumption.

Welcome to the terrifying, fascinating world of side-channel attacks on IMDs—where medical security meets high-tech espionage, and our own bodies become attack surfaces. Let's dive in.

1. What Are Side-Channel Attacks?

Side-channel attacks don't exploit a software vulnerability or break encryption directly. Instead, they use unintended information leaks to infer sensitive data. It's like eavesdropping on a conversation by analyzing someone's facial expressions instead of listening to their words.

For IMDs, side-channel attacks can involve:

◆ **Electromagnetic (EM) Emanations** – Capturing weak signals from an implantable device to infer its operations.
◆ **Power Analysis** – Measuring tiny fluctuations in power consumption to extract encryption keys.
◆ **Acoustic Side-Channels** – Using sound or vibrations from the device's components to infer data.

◆ **Timing Attacks** – Observing how long specific operations take to uncover sensitive information.

Since IMDs constantly transmit and process signals, they unknowingly leak information, making them juicy targets for attackers.

🔬 **Example Attack**: Researchers demonstrated that by analyzing electromagnetic emissions from a pacemaker, they could reconstruct the signals controlling heart rhythms—without needing to hack into the device directly.

2. Electromagnetic Attacks: When IMDs Talk Too Loud

Every electronic device gives off electromagnetic (EM) signals—and implantable medical devices are no exception. Skilled attackers can pick up these weak signals using sensitive antennas and infer medical data without even touching the patient.

◆ **EM Side-Channel Analysis** – Attackers analyze radiation from IMDs to extract encryption keys or operational states.
◆ **Fault Injection Attacks** – By blasting a device with controlled EM pulses, hackers can glitch its behavior, potentially causing it to malfunction or leak data.
◆ **Wireless Snooping** – Some IMDs use unencrypted or weakly encrypted RF communication, allowing attackers to listen in.

🔬 **Example Attack**: A team of researchers intercepted unencrypted transmissions from older pacemakers, allowing them to wirelessly extract patient data and even send unauthorized commands.

🔒 **Defense Strategy:**

✓ Use shielding techniques to reduce EM leaks.

✓ Implement stronger encryption on all wireless communications.

✓ Design IMDs with tamper-resistant hardware that prevents signal interception.

3. Power Analysis Attacks: Measuring Tiny Clues

Power consumption in IMDs is extremely low—but it's not zero. Even minuscule fluctuations can reveal secrets.

◆ **Simple Power Analysis (SPA):** Observing power usage patterns to determine what the device is doing.

◆ **Differential Power Analysis (DPA):** Collecting multiple power traces to extract cryptographic keys.

◆ **Battery Drain Attacks:** Attackers can force an IMD into a high-power consumption state, draining its battery years ahead of schedule.

🔍 **Example Attack**: Researchers showed that by analyzing power fluctuations in insulin pumps, they could infer how much insulin was being delivered—without directly hacking into the device.

🔒 **Defense Strategy:**

✔ Implement constant-power cryptographic operations to prevent power-based inference.

✔ Use randomized execution timing to mask operations.

✔ Design IMDs with tamper-detection circuits that shut down under abnormal power conditions.

4. Acoustic & Vibration Attacks: Hacking with Sound

Yes, attackers can even extract information just by listening to an IMD's tiny internal vibrations.

◆ **Microphone-Based Side-Channel Attacks** – Sound waves emitted by electrical components can be recorded and analyzed.

◆ **Vibration Attacks** – IMDs generate small mechanical vibrations that could theoretically be picked up by specialized sensors.

🔍 **Example Attack**: Scientists showed that ultrasonic waves could manipulate the pressure sensors inside insulin pumps, tricking them into delivering too much or too little insulin.

🔒 **Defense Strategy:**

✔ Shield IMDs from external acoustic interference.

✓ Use error-correcting algorithms to prevent false signals.

✓ Implement tamper-proof enclosures for internal components.

5. Timing Attacks: When Every Millisecond Counts

Attackers can figure out what an IMD is doing just by measuring how long operations take. This technique is often used to break encryption or detect specific medical states.

📖 **Example Attack**: By measuring timing variations in pacemaker responses, researchers could predict heart rate adjustments without direct access to the device.

🔒 **Defense Strategy:**

✓ Use constant-time cryptographic operations to prevent timing leaks.

✓ Randomize execution delays to make attacks harder.

✓ Minimize external interactions that could reveal timing data.

The Grim Reality: IMDs Are Hard to Secure

The problem with implantable medical devices is they aren't designed for frequent updates. Unlike your phone, which gets software patches regularly, IMDs may stay in a patient's body for 10+ years.

◆ Many IMDs use legacy encryption because their processors are too weak for modern security measures.
◆ Some manufacturers don't prioritize cybersecurity, focusing instead on FDA compliance.
◆ Wireless reprogramming features, designed for convenience, open doors to remote exploitation.

📖 **Case Study**: In 2017, the FDA issued a recall for over 465,000 pacemakers due to critical security vulnerabilities that could allow attackers to remotely reprogram them. That's nearly half a million people walking around with hackable hearts.

Final Thoughts: Are We Safe?

The idea of a hacker controlling an IMD remotely is terrifying, but it's also a real and growing risk. Side-channel attacks are just one of many ways attackers can exploit these life-saving devices.

◆ If manufacturers don't prioritize security, we're heading toward a future where medical cyberattacks could become a serious threat.
◆ The medical field needs stronger encryption, better shielding, and real-time monitoring to detect suspicious activity.
◆ Patients and doctors need to demand security updates and push manufacturers to take cybersecurity as seriously as they take medical efficacy.

So, if you ever find yourself getting a life-saving implant, maybe ask your doctor if it comes with a firewall. ☺

9.4 Reverse Engineering Medical Hardware for Exploitation

Breaking Medical Hardware: Because Why Should Hackers Have All the Fun?
Let's be honest—medical devices were never meant to be tampered with. The manufacturers don't want you poking around inside their multi-thousand-dollar pacemakers, insulin pumps, or neurostimulators. But as security professionals (or ethical hackers, if we're feeling fancy), we have one simple rule:

☞ If it has a chip, it can be hacked.

Reverse engineering medical hardware isn't just a fun challenge—it's a critical step in securing devices that millions of people rely on to stay alive. We're talking about the medical IoT (MIoT) devices that live inside us, monitor our vitals, and administer life-saving treatments. If a hacker can figure out how they work, so can we. And the stakes? Well, let's just say that "hackable pacemaker" sounds like a bad James Bond plot, except it's terrifyingly real.

1. Why Reverse Engineer Medical Hardware?

Most people take their medical devices at face value:

◆ **Pacemaker**? "It keeps my heart beating."
◆ **Insulin pump**? "It gives me the right dose."

◆ **Neurostimulator**? "It helps manage my pain."

But a hacker sees something different:

◆ **Pacemaker**? "It's a tiny embedded system that communicates over RF."
◆ **Insulin pump**? "It has firmware that might have hardcoded credentials."
◆ **Neurostimulator**? "It runs proprietary code that can be dumped and modified."

Reverse engineering lets us:

✓ Find vulnerabilities in proprietary firmware and hardware.

✓ Discover undocumented features (backdoors, debug modes, and admin interfaces).

✓ Test security measures like encryption, authentication, and firmware updates.

✓ Identify potential exploits before bad actors do.

And let's be clear: if a hacker finds a flaw before we do, bad things happen.

2. The Hardware Hacking Toolkit for Medical Devices

Reverse engineering medical hardware requires a blend of traditional hacking skills and specialized tools. Here's what's in our bag of tricks:

◆ **JTAG/SWD Debuggers** – Used to interface with embedded processors and extract firmware.
◆ **Bus Analyzers (SPI, I2C, UART, CAN)** – Helps intercept communication between components.
◆ **RF Sniffers (HackRF, RTL-SDR, Proxmark3)** – Captures wireless signals from implantable and external devices.
◆ **Oscilloscopes & Logic Analyzers** – Detects electrical signals and reverse-engineers circuit behavior.
◆ **Chip-Off Techniques** – Extracts firmware directly from memory chips using heat or chemicals.
◆ **Disassemblers & Decompilers (Ghidra, IDA Pro, Radare2)** – Turns binary code into human-readable assembly.

If all that sounds intimidating, don't worry—we're going to break it down.

3. Extracting Firmware: The First Step to Total Control

Firmware is where the magic happens in medical IoT devices. It's the brains of the operation, dictating how the device processes data, communicates, and responds to commands.

How to Dump Firmware from a Medical Device:

1☐ **Find a Debug Interface** – Many medical devices have JTAG or SWD ports left open.

2☐ **Connect a Debugger** – Use a JTAGulator or Bus Pirate to interface with the chip.

3☐ **Dump the Firmware** – Extract the binary and analyze it with Ghidra or IDA Pro.

4☐ **Search for Secrets** – Look for hardcoded credentials, encryption keys, and hidden commands.

🔟 **Example Attack**: Researchers found that some older pacemakers had hardcoded administrator passwords, allowing attackers to wirelessly modify device settings. The kicker? The passwords were the same across all devices.

🔒 **Defense Strategy:**

✓ Disable unused debug interfaces in production devices.

✓ Implement secure boot to prevent unauthorized firmware modifications.

✓ Use encrypted firmware updates to prevent tampering.

4. Sniffing RF Communication: Wireless Hacking 101

Many medical devices communicate wirelessly—either with an external controller, a hospital network, or another implanted device. This radio chatter is a goldmine for attackers.

How Hackers Intercept Medical Device RF Signals:

1☐ **Identify the Frequency** – Use a software-defined radio (SDR) to scan for signals.

2☐ **Capture Transmissions** – Tools like HackRF or RTL-SDR can record raw RF traffic.

3☐ **Analyze Protocols** – Look for unencrypted data or predictable patterns.

4️⃣ **Replay or Modify Signals** – Attackers can spoof commands or disrupt communication.

📛 **Example Attack**: Security researchers intercepted wireless transmissions from insulin pumps and sent fake commands to alter dosage levels. No hacking into the device required—just RF manipulation.

🔒 **Defense Strategy:**

✅ Encrypt all wireless transmissions to prevent eavesdropping.

✅ Implement replay attack protections to reject old or modified commands.

✅ Use frequency hopping to make interception harder.

5. Dumping Memory & Extracting Sensitive Data

IMDs store sensitive data, including encryption keys, medical history, and device configurations. Attackers can extract this data using chip-off techniques or side-channel attacks.

How Hackers Dump Memory from Medical Devices:

1️⃣ **Identify the Memory Chip** – EEPROM, Flash, or SRAM?

2️⃣ **Extract the Chip** – Using heat, chemicals, or a precision soldering station.

3️⃣ **Dump the Data** – Read the raw memory using SPI or I2C adapters.

4️⃣ **Analyze the Contents** – Search for unencrypted patient data or cryptographic secrets.

📛 **Example Attack**: Some older pacemakers stored unencrypted patient data in easily accessible flash memory, allowing attackers to extract private medical history.

🔒 **Defense Strategy:**

✅ Encrypt sensitive data at rest to prevent unauthorized access.

✅ Use secure enclaves to store cryptographic keys separately.

✅ Implement tamper-detection circuits that wipe memory if an attack is detected.

Final Thoughts: Why This Matters

Medical hardware isn't just about cool hacks and technical wizardry—it's about protecting real people from real threats. If a hacker can reverse-engineer a pacemaker or insulin pump, they can potentially control someone's life-supporting device remotely.

We're at a critical point in medical cybersecurity. Manufacturers need to start treating security as important as patient safety, and ethical hackers need to stay one step ahead of the bad guys.

So the next time you see a pacemaker, an insulin pump, or a neurostimulator, ask yourself:

Would you trust this device with your life if you knew how easy it was to hack?

If the answer is no, we've got work to do. 💀

9.5 Hardening Physical Security for Medical IoT Devices

Because Duct Tape Won't Fix This

Let's be real—if someone can physically touch a device, it's already half-hacked. This isn't just a cybersecurity issue; it's a physical security problem. We can encrypt, firewall, and patch software all day long, but if an attacker can pick up, open, or steal a device, they can usually bypass everything we've done to protect it.

Imagine a hacker disguised as a janitor strolling into a hospital, swiping a smart infusion pump, and walking out like they just grabbed a coffee. No exploits, no zero-days—just five fingers and a lack of proper security controls.

When it comes to Medical IoT (MIoT) devices, physical security isn't optional. Whether it's a wearable health tracker, an implantable pacemaker, or a networked medical workstation, we need strong defenses against theft, tampering, and unauthorized access.

1. The Problem: Physical Attacks on Medical IoT Devices

Attackers don't always need a laptop and fancy tools. Sometimes, they just need physical access to a device to:

✅ **Steal it** – Portable medical devices (wearables, insulin pumps, portable monitors) are easy targets for theft.

✅ **Tamper with it** – Attackers can open, modify, or replace components to introduce backdoors.

✅ **Extract Data** – Many devices store unencrypted patient data that can be dumped from memory chips.

✅ **Bypass Authentication** – If a device has debug ports, exposed connectors, or removable storage, an attacker can bypass security checks entirely.

🔊 **Real-World Example**: Researchers found that certain hospital MRI machines had default passwords printed on the manufacturer's label—literally on the back of the device. No hacking required—just turn it around and read.

2. Hardening Medical Devices Against Physical Attacks

We need to think like an attacker and ask: If I could touch this device, how would I break it?

A. Preventing Unauthorized Access

🔒 **Lock it down**: Use tamper-resistant enclosures for standalone medical devices. If an attacker can't open it without breaking it, they'll think twice.

🔒 **Disable debug ports**: JTAG, UART, SPI—these are goldmines for attackers. If you don't need them, disable them or use strong authentication.

🔒 **Secure remote access**: If a device must connect remotely, require multi-factor authentication (MFA) to prevent unauthorized logins.

B. Protecting Internal Components

🔒 **Chip Security**: Implement secure boot so attackers can't flash unauthorized firmware. Use encrypted storage for sensitive patient data.

🔒 **Tamper Detection**: Many financial devices (like ATMs) have tamper-resistant circuits that wipe memory if someone tries to open them. Why don't medical devices?

🔒 **Glue it, screw it, shield it**: Exposed memory chips and debug headers? Epoxy them shut or use metal shielding to make attacks harder.

📟 **Real-World Example**: Some older pacemakers stored patient data in plaintext on an easily removable memory chip. An attacker could pop open the device, pull the chip, and read it with an off-the-shelf programmer. That's not hacking—that's just bad security.

3. Protecting Against Theft & Unauthorized Removal

Many medical IoT devices are small, portable, and easy to steal. If they're not properly secured, they can disappear faster than a free donut in a hospital break room.

A. Anti-Theft Measures for Medical Devices

🔒 **Physical Locks**: If a device is stationary (like a smart hospital bed or workstation), lock it down with cables, brackets, or security screws.

🔒 **Location Tracking**: Use GPS or RFID-based asset tracking for high-value medical devices. If one goes missing, you'll know before it ends up on eBay.

🔒 **Proximity Alarms**: If a device is removed from a secure area, set off an alarm or send an alert to hospital security.

📟 **Real-World Example**: In 2022, a hacker stole a smart infusion pump from a hospital and later discovered unencrypted Wi-Fi credentials stored inside. The hospital's entire network was compromised—all because a single device walked out the door.

4. Defending Against Physical Tampering & Side-Channel Attacks

Even if a device stays inside a hospital, an attacker could tamper with it to modify its behavior or extract data.

A. Hardware-Based Security Measures

🔒 **Tamper-Proof Screws & Seals**: Basic, but effective. If a device has custom security screws or tamper-evident seals, attackers can't open it without leaving evidence.

🔒 **Side-Channel Attack Defenses**: Implantable medical devices (IMDs) can be vulnerable to electromagnetic and power analysis attacks. Shielding can help prevent attackers from reading signals remotely.

🔒 **Anti-Tamper Switches**: Some high-security devices erase sensitive data if tampering is detected. Why don't all life-critical devices have this?

🔍 **Real-World Example**: A security researcher demonstrated that an attacker could use electromagnetic pulses to disrupt the operation of a pacemaker without ever touching it. That's some James Bond-level hacking, but the risk is real.

5. Secure Disposal & Decommissioning of Medical Devices

Even when a device is no longer in use, it can still be a security risk. Why? Because old medical devices often store sensitive patient data—and many hospitals don't properly wipe them before disposal.

A. Secure Disposal Practices

☐ **Factory Reset Before Disposal**: Ensure all devices undergo a secure factory reset to remove patient data.

☐ **Physical Destruction**: If a device stores critical patient data, consider shredding, incinerating, or physically destroying memory chips.

☐ **Proper Decommissioning Policies**: Hospitals should have strict protocols for decommissioning and disposing of medical devices.

🔍 **Real-World Example**: A hospital once sold used medical devices on an auction site—without wiping them. The buyer found thousands of patient records still stored on the machines. Oops.

Final Thoughts: Physical Security is Cybersecurity

At the end of the day, if an attacker can touch it, they can hack it. Good security isn't just about firewalls and encryption—it's about making sure devices are physically protected, too.

So, what's the lesson here? If you work in medical cybersecurity, stop thinking like an IT person for a second. Instead, think like a thief, a hacker, or a rogue hospital worker. Look at every medical device and ask:

- Can I steal it?
- Can I open it?
- Can I tamper with it without getting caught?

If the answer is yes to any of those questions, fix it before someone else exploits it. Because in the world of medical IoT, the stakes aren't just financial—they're human lives.

Chapter 10: Securing the Future of Medical IoT

Let's face it—Medical IoT security is a mess. But it doesn't have to stay that way. The good news? Researchers, ethical hackers, and security professionals are working hard to fix the problem. The bad news? Attackers aren't slowing down either. The future of smart healthcare depends on how well we secure these systems now.

This final chapter discusses best practices for strengthening medical IoT security, from secure firmware updates to AI-powered threat detection. We'll explore privacy concerns, regulatory improvements, and emerging threats in healthcare cybersecurity. By implementing proactive security measures today, we can ensure a safer, more resilient future for connected healthcare.

10.1 Best Practices for Medical IoT Security Hardening

Why Security Isn't Just an Afterthought (or a Patch After a Breach)

Let's be honest—medical IoT security is a hot mess. Hospitals are running decade-old systems, devices are riddled with vulnerabilities, and hackers love easy targets (especially the kind that don't update their firmware). If you're reading this, you probably care about securing medical IoT—or at least preventing your hospital from making headlines for all the wrong reasons.

So, how do we fix this? The good news: it's possible. The bad news? There's no single magic fix. Security hardening is all about layered defense, best practices, and actually implementing them (because a security policy nobody follows is just a really boring novel).

1. Implement Strong Authentication and Access Controls

One of the biggest problems in medical IoT security is bad authentication. Weak or default passwords make it stupidly easy for attackers to compromise devices. (Looking at you, hospitals still using "admin123" for your smart infusion pumps).

A. Enforce Strong Password Policies

🔒 **No default passwords** – Require unique, randomized credentials for every medical IoT device.

🔒 **Enforce MFA (Multi-Factor Authentication)** – A password alone isn't enough; require a second form of authentication.

🔒 **Use role-based access controls (RBAC)** – Not everyone should have admin access to every device.

📢 **Real-World Fail**: In 2021, researchers found thousands of infusion pumps online using default login credentials. Hackers could literally control medication dosages remotely. Let's not let that happen again.

2. Secure Medical IoT Firmware and Software

If your device is still running 2015 firmware, congratulations! You're an easy target for hackers. Keeping firmware and software updated is critical for security.

A. Implement Secure Firmware Updates

🔒 **Digitally sign all firmware updates** – Prevent attackers from pushing malicious firmware.

🔒 **Use encrypted update delivery** – Ensure updates are secure and can't be intercepted.

🔒 **Require authentication for updates** – Only authorized personnel should be able to install them.

📢 **Real-World Fail**: Some smart pacemakers had no authentication for updates, meaning anyone within range could potentially push malicious firmware. Yeah, that's terrifying.

3. Encrypt Everything (Because Plaintext Data is a Gift to Hackers)

Medical IoT devices transmit and store sensitive patient data. If it's not encrypted, hackers will steal it.

A. Data Encryption Best Practices

🔒 **Encrypt data at rest** – Any patient data stored on a device should be encrypted.

🔒 **Encrypt data in transit** – Use TLS 1.2 or 1.3 for secure communication.

🔒 **Avoid hardcoded cryptographic keys** – If your encryption key is baked into firmware, you're doing it wrong.

🔒 **Real-World Fail**: A major hospital suffered a breach because their patient monitoring devices stored data in plaintext—which an attacker accessed via an unprotected network port. Oops.

4. Network Segmentation: Because IoT and Patient Records Shouldn't Mix

A flat hospital network is a hacker's playground. If your MRI machine is on the same network as the billing system, attackers only need to breach one device to move laterally.

A. Proper Network Segmentation Strategies

🔒 **Separate IoT devices from critical hospital systems** – Use VLANs to isolate MIoT devices.
🔒 **Implement Zero Trust Architecture (ZTA)** – No device should be trusted by default.
🔒 **Use firewalls and intrusion detection** – Monitor and block unauthorized traffic.

🔒 **Real-World Fail**: WannaCry ransomware spread like wildfire in hospitals because medical devices weren't segmented from the main network. Don't let history repeat itself.

5. Monitor, Detect, and Respond to Threats

You can't stop an attack if you don't know it's happening. Many hospitals lack real-time monitoring of medical IoT devices, which means they don't notice breaches until it's too late.

A. Security Monitoring Best Practices

🔒 **Deploy an IoT-specific SIEM** (Security Information and Event Management) solution – You need visibility into every device.
🔒 **Set up anomaly detection** – If a smart heart monitor suddenly starts making network connections to China, that's a problem.
🔒 **Log everything** – If you don't log it, you won't know what happened after an attack.

🔒 **Real-World Fail**: In 2020, an IoT security firm found hundreds of medical devices communicating with known malicious IP addresses—and the hospitals had no idea.

6. Implement Secure API and Cloud Practices

Many medical IoT devices connect to the cloud, but weak API security is an open invitation for hackers.

A. API and Cloud Security Best Practices

🔒 **Enforce strong authentication for APIs** – No open, unauthenticated API endpoints.

🔒 **Use rate limiting** – Prevent brute-force and DDoS attacks on healthcare APIs.

🔒 **Encrypt cloud storage** – Patient data should be encrypted before it even reaches the cloud.

🔎 **Real-World Fail**: A telemedicine app exposed thousands of patient records because its API lacked authentication. Hackers didn't need an exploit—they just visited the API in a browser.

7. Secure Physical Access to Devices

Even the best cybersecurity measures won't matter if an attacker can just walk into a hospital and steal a device.

A. Physical Security Best Practices

🔒 **Use tamper-resistant enclosures** – If an attacker can't open the device, they can't tamper with it.

🔒 **Disable debug ports** – JTAG, UART, SPI—if you don't need them, lock them down.

🔒 **Implement geofencing and tracking** – If a device leaves a secure zone, alert security.

🔎 **Real-World Fail**: A hacker stole a smart infusion pump from a hospital, took it home, and found the hospital's Wi-Fi credentials stored inside. One stolen device = full network access.

Final Thoughts: Security Hardening is an Ongoing Process

Medical IoT security isn't a one-and-done thing. Hackers evolve, technology evolves, and security needs to evolve too.

💡 **Remember:**

✓ **Use strong authentication** – No more default passwords.

✓ **Encrypt everything** – If it's sensitive, encrypt it.

✓ **Segment networks** – IoT devices shouldn't talk to critical systems.

✓ **Monitor and detect threats** – If you're not watching, you're already compromised.

✓ **Lock down physical access** – If someone can touch it, they can hack it.

● **Bottom line**: Medical IoT saves lives, but poor security risks them. If you work in healthcare IT, your job isn't just to keep devices running—it's to keep people safe.

And if all else fails? Just don't be the next hospital making headlines for a ransomware attack. ☐

10.2 Implementing Secure Firmware Updates and Patch Management

Why Updating Medical IoT Devices Feels Like Herding Cats

Let's get real for a second—nobody likes updates. We've all ignored that "Update Available" notification more times than we'd like to admit. But when it comes to medical IoT devices, ignoring updates isn't just annoying—it's downright dangerous. A single unpatched vulnerability in a smart infusion pump, pacemaker, or MRI machine can be an open invitation for hackers.

So why don't hospitals just update everything? Well, firmware updates in medical IoT aren't as simple as hitting "Install" on your phone. Compatibility issues, regulatory concerns, and the dreaded "if it ain't broke, don't fix it" mindset all make updates a logistical nightmare. But here's the truth: not updating is a bigger risk than updating. Let's dive into how to do firmware updates and patch management the right way—without breaking devices (or causing a hospital-wide panic).

1. The Challenges of Firmware Updates in Medical IoT

Updating medical IoT firmware isn't like updating your laptop. A single mistake can brick a life-critical device or, worse, introduce new security risks. Some key challenges include:

A. Downtime and Availability Issues

⊕ **Medical devices can't afford downtime** – Unlike a smartphone update, you can't just reboot a ventilator mid-surgery.

⊕ **Many hospitals run 24/7** – Finding a maintenance window is tricky, and some devices never go offline.

B. Regulatory and Compliance Hurdles

⚖☐ Regulatory approvals (FDA, IEC 62304) can delay firmware patches for months or even years.

⚖☐ Some devices require recertification after updates, making manufacturers hesitant to release patches frequently.

C. Compatibility and Legacy System Nightmares

💾 **Some hospitals still run Windows XP (yes, seriously)** – New firmware updates might not be compatible with ancient infrastructure.

💾 Different devices from different manufacturers don't always play nicely together, leading to unexpected failures.

⚖ **Real-World Fail**: A major hospital network delayed a firmware update for wireless infusion pumps because they feared compatibility issues. Months later, hackers exploited the unpatched flaw, gaining remote control over medication dosages.

2. Best Practices for Secure Firmware Updates

Now that we know why firmware updates are a pain, let's talk about how to do them securely and efficiently.

A. Digitally Sign and Authenticate All Firmware Updates

🔒 **Use cryptographic signatures** – Firmware updates should be signed with a private key so only legitimate updates can be installed.

🔒 **Verify updates before installation** – Devices should check for tampering before applying an update.

⚖ **Real-World Fail**: Some medical IoT devices have no verification mechanism, meaning attackers can install malicious firmware by intercepting an update.

B. Encrypt Update Files and Secure Transmission

🔒 **Encrypt firmware files** – Prevent attackers from reverse-engineering the update to find vulnerabilities.

🔒 **Use secure transport (TLS 1.2 or 1.3)** – Updates should be downloaded over encrypted connections, not HTTP or FTP.

📟 **Real-World Fail**: Researchers found unprotected firmware update servers, allowing attackers to download and modify firmware before it reached devices.

C. Implement Rollback Protection and Fail-Safe Mechanisms

🔒 **Prevent downgrades** – Attackers love exploiting older, vulnerable firmware versions. Devices should reject outdated updates.

🔒 **Implement fail-safe recovery** – If an update fails, the device should revert to a stable version instead of becoming a very expensive brick.

📟 **Real-World Fail**: Some medical IoT devices allow firmware downgrades, making it easy for attackers to reintroduce old vulnerabilities.

3. Effective Patch Management Strategies

Firmware updates are just one part of the equation—you also need a solid patch management strategy. Here's how to do it right:

A. Implement an Automated Patch Management System

✅ **Use centralized patch management tools** – Hospitals should have one system managing updates for all devices.

✅ **Schedule updates strategically** – Apply patches during low-risk hours to minimize disruptions.

📟 **Real-World Fail**: Many hospitals still manually update devices, leading to months-long delays in patching critical vulnerabilities.

B. Prioritize Patches Based on Risk

✅ **Not all patches are equal** – Focus on high-risk vulnerabilities first (e.g., remote code execution flaws).

✅ **Use threat intelligence** – Stay updated on newly discovered medical IoT vulnerabilities.

🚨 **Real-World Fail**: Some hospitals apply updates alphabetically rather than by risk level. (Yes, really.)

C. Maintain a Firmware and Patch Inventory

✅ **Track all devices and firmware versions** – You can't patch what you don't know exists.
✅ **Ensure vendor support** – If a device is no longer receiving updates, it's time to replace it.

🚨 **Real-World Fail**: A healthcare provider was hit by ransomware because they didn't realize some of their MRI machines were running outdated firmware.

4. Overcoming Resistance to Firmware Updates

Let's face it—people hate updates. IT teams worry about breaking devices, and doctors just want their machines to work. Here's how to get everyone on board with firmware security.

A. Educate Healthcare Staff on the Importance of Updates

🧑‍💻 **Explain that unpatched devices = security risk** – Hackers love hospitals because they're slow to patch.
🧑‍💻 **Provide simple, non-technical explanations** – No one wants a 50-page cybersecurity lecture.

🚨 **Real-World Fail**: A hospital delayed a firmware update for an entire year because staff didn't understand why it was necessary.

B. Work with Vendors to Improve Update Processes

☐ **Push for timely patches** – If a vendor takes forever to release updates, pressure them to improve.
☐ **Demand transparency** – Medical device manufacturers should disclose vulnerabilities and provide clear update instructions.

🏛 **Real-World Fail**: Some vendors hide vulnerabilities instead of fixing them, leaving hospitals exposed to attacks.

Final Thoughts: Firmware Updates Aren't Optional

If there's one takeaway from this chapter, it's this: ignoring firmware updates is like leaving your front door open in a bad neighborhood.

💡 **Key Takeaways:**

✅ **Always verify and sign firmware updates** – No unsigned or unauthenticated updates allowed.

✅ **Encrypt updates and use secure transport** – No plaintext firmware files floating around.

✅ **Have a rollback plan** – If an update fails, the device shouldn't die.

✅ **Patch based on risk, not random order** – Focus on critical security flaws first.

✅ **Educate staff and pressure vendors** – Updates need buy-in from everyone.

⬤ **Bottom line**: In the world of medical IoT, firmware updates can save lives—or cost them if done wrong. If you're in charge of securing medical IoT, your job isn't just about keeping devices running—it's about keeping people safe.

So, next time you see a firmware update notification, don't ignore it. It might just be the thing standing between your hospital and the next big cyberattack. ☐

10.3 Role of AI and Machine Learning in Medical IoT Threat Detection

Can AI Save Us from Hackers—or Will It Just Recommend a Diet Plan?

Artificial Intelligence (AI) is everywhere—from recommending movies you'll never watch to sending you guilt-inducing fitness notifications. But can AI actually protect hospitals and medical IoT devices from cyberattacks? Well, that depends. AI can be a powerful security ally or a glorified Clippy from Microsoft Word, depending on how it's implemented.

With hospitals facing an onslaught of cyber threats, from ransomware attacks on MRI machines to hackers remotely controlling insulin pumps, traditional security measures just aren't enough. That's where AI-driven threat detection comes in. AI and Machine Learning (ML) can spot threats faster than humans, detect anomalies in real time, and even predict cyberattacks before they happen. But let's not pretend it's magic—AI has its own challenges and limitations. So, let's break down how AI and ML are transforming medical IoT security—and whether we should be excited or terrified.

1. How AI and ML Are Used in Medical IoT Threat Detection

AI isn't just for self-driving cars and robotic surgeons—it's also playing a major role in identifying and mitigating cyber threats in healthcare environments. Here's how:

A. Real-Time Anomaly Detection

☐ AI continuously monitors network traffic, device behavior, and system logs for anything suspicious.
☐ Unlike traditional security systems, ML models adapt over time, recognizing new attack patterns before they cause damage.

🔬 **Example**: AI detects an MRI machine suddenly transmitting large amounts of data to an unknown server. Instead of waiting for IT to notice, the AI flags it instantly and blocks the connection.

B. Predictive Threat Analysis

🔍 AI can predict future attacks based on historical data and attack patterns.
🔍 This helps security teams stay ahead of hackers rather than always reacting after a breach.

🔬 **Example**: AI notices multiple failed login attempts on a hospital's telemedicine portal, correlates it with previous attack patterns, and alerts IT before an actual breach occurs.

C. Automated Response and Incident Containment

☐ AI can automate incident response, isolating infected devices before malware spreads across the hospital network.
☐ This is crucial for stopping ransomware attacks, which can cripple entire healthcare systems within minutes.

🔒 **Example**: A hacker attempts to deploy ransomware on a hospital's cloud-connected infusion pumps. AI detects the anomaly, disconnects the infected devices, and triggers an alert—all within seconds.

2. Challenges of AI in Medical IoT Security

AI isn't perfect (yet). While it enhances security, it also comes with some major challenges that hospitals and IT teams need to consider.

A. False Positives and Alert Fatigue

🔒 AI can sometimes be too sensitive, flagging benign activity as a cyber threat.
🔒 Too many false alarms = IT teams start ignoring alerts, which defeats the whole purpose.

💡 **Solution**: Fine-tune AI models using real-world medical IoT data to reduce false positives.

B. AI Models Can Be Tricked (Adversarial Attacks)

🎭 Hackers can manipulate AI models using adversarial inputs—feeding them slightly modified data to bypass detection.
🎭 **Example**: An attacker slightly modifies ransomware signatures so the AI doesn't recognize it as a threat.

💡 **Solution**: Use continuous retraining and adaptive learning to harden AI models against adversarial attacks.

C. Data Privacy and Compliance Issues

📋 AI requires huge amounts of data to function effectively, but in healthcare, data privacy is a legal minefield.
📋 Regulations like HIPAA and GDPR impose strict rules on data usage and patient confidentiality.

💡 **Solution**: Implement privacy-preserving AI techniques like federated learning, which allows AI to learn without exposing sensitive patient data.

3. Best Practices for Implementing AI in Medical IoT Security

A. Train AI Models Using Healthcare-Specific Threat Data

✓ AI should be trained on real medical IoT threats, not just generic cybersecurity threats.

✓ Hospitals should collaborate with cybersecurity firms to build better AI-driven security solutions.

B. Use AI for Continuous Monitoring and Response

✓ AI shouldn't replace human security teams—it should augment them.

✓ Implement AI-driven Security Operations Centers (SOCs) for 24/7 monitoring of medical IoT devices.

C. Ensure AI Systems Follow Compliance Guidelines

✓ AI-driven security solutions must comply with HIPAA, FDA, and IEC 62304 regulations.

✓ Implement explainable AI (XAI) so that security teams understand why AI flagged an incident.

4. The Future of AI in Medical IoT Security

AI isn't a silver bullet, but it is a game-changer. As cyberattacks on hospitals continue to rise, AI will become a core component of medical IoT security. Here's what's coming next:

🔧 **Self-Healing IoT Devices** – AI-driven systems that can detect, isolate, and patch vulnerabilities automatically.

🔧 **AI-Powered Digital Twins** – Virtual replicas of hospital networks used to simulate attacks and test defenses in real-time.

🔧 **More Sophisticated AI-Powered Attacks** – Just as defenders use AI, hackers are developing AI-driven attack tools—creating a never-ending cyber arms race.

Final Thoughts: AI – A Friend or a Future Overlord?

AI in medical IoT security is like having an overprotective robot assistant—sometimes helpful, sometimes annoying, but always necessary. While it won't eliminate cyber threats entirely, it can detect, predict, and respond to them faster than any human.

💡 Key Takeaways:

✅ AI detects anomalies and cyber threats in real time, making hospitals more resilient against attacks.

✅ AI can predict and prevent cyberattacks, but needs constant fine-tuning to avoid false alarms.

✅ AI must comply with medical regulations to ensure patient data privacy.

✅ Hackers are developing AI-driven attacks, so hospitals must stay ahead with smarter AI defenses.

At the end of the day, AI is a powerful tool—but just like a scalpel in the hands of a surgeon, it needs to be used correctly. So, should hospitals embrace AI for IoT security? Absolutely. Just don't be surprised if it starts recommending yoga and kale smoothies while defending your MRI machine. 😄

10.4 Privacy Concerns and Patient Data Protection Strategies

Your Medical Data Is Worth More Than You Think—And Hackers Know It

Imagine you walk into a hospital, get a check-up, and go home. A few days later, you start receiving weird emails: "Hey [Your Name], we noticed your blood pressure was a little high last week. How about a special offer on hypertension meds?" Creepy, right? Welcome to the wild world of medical data privacy—or the lack of it.

Your medical records are worth more than your credit card number on the dark web. A stolen healthcare record can sell for up to 50 times more than financial data because it includes everything—your name, birth date, Social Security number, prescriptions, insurance details, and even embarrassing diagnoses (looking at you, unexpected rash). Hackers, data brokers, and even some shady organizations are hungry for this information. The question is: how do we protect it?

Let's break down the biggest privacy concerns in smart healthcare and how we can actually keep patient data safe before it ends up fueling the next big ransomware attack.

1. Why Medical Data Privacy Matters More Than Ever

Medical IoT devices collect, transmit, and store an insane amount of sensitive data. From wearable fitness trackers to implantable pacemakers and smart hospital beds, everything is connected to the cloud—and that means everything is a target.

Here's why privacy breaches in healthcare are a massive problem:

A. Identity Theft and Fraud

- A hacked medical record can be used to steal your identity, open fake insurance claims, or even get prescription drugs in your name.
- Unlike a stolen credit card (which you can cancel), you can't "cancel" your medical history—once it's out, it's out.

B. Ransomware and Extortion

- Hackers lock down hospital systems and demand huge ransoms to restore access—delaying life-saving treatments.
- Some cybercriminals go further, threatening to leak sensitive patient data unless they get paid.

C. Data Selling and Exploitation

- Unethical data brokers collect and sell patient data to advertisers, insurance companies, or even employers.
- This can lead to higher insurance premiums or job discrimination based on health history (yes, it happens).

2. The Biggest Privacy Risks in Medical IoT

Okay, so we know why privacy matters. Now let's talk about how medical IoT devices are making things worse.

A. Unsecured Wearables and Remote Monitoring Devices

- Smartwatches, fitness trackers, and heart monitors continuously collect health data—but many have weak encryption (or none at all).
- Hackers can intercept data from Bluetooth and Wi-Fi connections, exposing sensitive patient details.

B. Weak Cloud Security in Healthcare Networks

- Many hospitals store patient records in cloud-based systems, but misconfigurations and weak authentication leave them vulnerable.
- A single cloud storage misconfiguration can expose millions of patient records to the internet.

C. Third-Party Medical Apps and APIs

- Many healthcare providers use third-party apps for telemedicine and patient data management—but not all apps follow strict security standards.
- If an API (application programming interface) is poorly secured, hackers can exploit it to access patient data.

3. How to Protect Patient Data in the Medical IoT Age

Now, for the good news: privacy isn't completely doomed—but it requires stronger security measures and smarter regulations.

A. Implement Stronger Encryption for Medical Data

- All patient data should be encrypted at rest and in transit—meaning even if hackers steal it, they can't read it.
- Use end-to-end encryption for telemedicine and remote patient monitoring systems.

B. Enforce Strict Access Controls

- Hospitals should use multi-factor authentication (MFA) for accessing medical records.
- Implement role-based access control (RBAC)—only authorized personnel should access certain patient data.

C. Secure Cloud Storage and Medical APIs

- Regularly audit and patch cloud storage configurations to prevent data leaks.
- Implement secure authentication (OAuth 2.0, token-based security) for medical APIs.

D. Educate Patients and Medical Staff on Privacy Risks

- Patients should know what data their devices collect and who has access.
- Healthcare workers should be trained on phishing scams, social engineering attacks, and data handling best practices.

E. Comply with Medical Data Protection Regulations

Healthcare organizations must follow strict privacy laws like:

HIPAA (USA) – Sets standards for patient data protection.

GDPR (Europe) – Protects patient data and gives individuals control over their information.

IEC 62304 – Security guidelines for medical device software development.

4. Future Trends in Medical Data Privacy

The fight for privacy isn't over—new technologies are emerging to keep patient data safer (or make things worse, depending on who you ask).

- **Blockchain-Based Medical Records** – Decentralized, tamper-proof medical records that patients control.
- **AI-Powered Privacy Monitoring** – AI that detects suspicious data access patterns in real-time.
- **Zero-Trust Architecture (ZTA)** – A security model where no one is automatically trusted—every device and user must be verified.

Final Thoughts: Should You Worry About Your Medical Data? (Yes, But Don't Panic)

Let's be real: privacy is a mess right now. Hackers are getting smarter, medical IoT devices are collecting more data than ever, and many healthcare providers are still playing catch-up.

But here's the good news: you don't have to be powerless. Hospitals, manufacturers, and even patients can take real steps to protect medical data. Encrypt everything, demand stronger security from medical device companies, and don't trust shady health apps that want access to your entire life history.

And if you ever get an email saying, "We know about your recent doctor's visit—click here to see your test results," just delete it and call your doctor instead.

10.5 Future Trends and Emerging Threats in Smart Healthcare Security

The Future of Medical IoT Security: More Gadgets, More Problems?

Picture this: It's 2035. Your smartwatch not only tracks your steps but also predicts your blood pressure, schedules doctor appointments, and even orders medication before you know you need it. Your pacemaker updates itself over Wi-Fi. Your AI-powered robotic surgeon schedules your hip replacement and asks if you'd like an upgrade while it's at it.

Sounds amazing, right? Well, now imagine a hacker intercepting that pacemaker update, tampering with your medication orders, or blackmailing patients by threatening to shut down their life-saving devices. Welcome to the future of medical IoT security—the good, the bad, and the terrifying.

Medical IoT (MIoT) is advancing at warp speed, and while it's revolutionizing healthcare, new security risks are evolving just as fast. In this chapter, we're diving into the emerging trends and threats that will shape the next decade of smart healthcare security.

1. The Rise of AI-Driven Healthcare and Its Security Risks

A. AI-Powered Diagnosis and Treatment

- AI systems are already analyzing X-rays, detecting diseases, and making treatment recommendations faster than human doctors.
- The problem? Hackers can manipulate AI models by feeding them poisoned data—causing misdiagnoses or incorrect prescriptions.

B. Deepfake Medical Scams

- Imagine receiving a video call from "your doctor" telling you to change your medication. Except... it's not your doctor—it's a deepfake created by cybercriminals.
- Deepfake-powered medical fraud and social engineering attacks are expected to skyrocket.

C. AI-Powered Cyberattacks

- AI isn't just helping doctors—it's also helping hackers.
- Malware is getting smarter and can now learn how to bypass security defenses on its own.

2. The Growing Threat of Ransomware 2.0 in Hospitals

A. Targeted Attacks on Life-Saving Equipment

- Traditional ransomware locks up hospital systems, but the next-gen versions will target IoT medical devices directly.
- Hackers could threaten to shut down ventilators, insulin pumps, or pacemakers unless hospitals pay up.

B. Ransomware-as-a-Service (RaaS) Expanding into Healthcare

- Cybercriminals are selling ready-made ransomware kits on the dark web.
- Even low-skill attackers can launch devastating ransomware attacks on hospitals for quick profit.

C. Cloud-Based Ransomware

- As hospitals move medical data to the cloud, ransomware will follow, targeting cloud storage and backups.

3. The Expansion of 5G and Edge Computing in Smart Healthcare

A. Ultra-Fast Connectivity = More Attack Surfaces

- 5G and edge computing enable real-time patient monitoring and faster medical data transfers—but they also introduce new vulnerabilities.
- Remote surgeries, connected ambulances, and smart hospitals will all rely on 5G, making network security critical.

B. Edge Devices Will Be a New Target

- Smart hospital equipment will process data locally (on edge devices) rather than in centralized cloud servers.
- These edge devices could be easier to hack than cloud-based systems.

4. Biometric and Implantable Device Exploits

A. Hacking Implantable Medical Devices (IMDs)

- Pacemakers, insulin pumps, and neurostimulators are now wirelessly updatable—which means they're also hackable.
- Future attacks could involve biohacking, where malicious actors manipulate smart implants to harm or control patients.

B. Biometric Data Theft

- Many hospitals now use fingerprints, facial recognition, and even retina scans for security.
- The problem? Biometric data can't be changed—if it gets stolen, it's permanently compromised.

5. Quantum Computing: The Next Security Nightmare

A. Quantum Computers Can Break Today's Encryption

- The encryption that protects patient data could be cracked in seconds by powerful quantum computers.
- Hospitals and medical device manufacturers must start preparing for quantum-resistant encryption NOW.

B. Quantum-Powered Security Solutions

- The good news? Quantum encryption (like quantum key distribution) will offer near-unbreakable security—if hospitals invest in it early.

6. Privacy Battles: Who Really Owns Your Health Data?

A. The Rise of Data Brokers Selling Medical Information

- Many smart health apps and devices collect patient data—and some sell it to advertisers, insurance companies, and even employers.
- Future regulations (like GDPR and HIPAA updates) must address this growing concern.

B. The Push for Patient-Controlled Health Data

- Emerging solutions (like blockchain-based health records) could give patients full control over their own data—instead of hospitals and corporations.

7. Future Defense Strategies for Medical IoT Security

- The threats are evolving, but so are the defenses. Here's how the healthcare industry can prepare:

A. Zero-Trust Security Models

- Never trust, always verify—every device, user, and system must be authenticated before accessing medical data.

B. AI-Driven Threat Detection

- AI security tools can monitor hospital networks and detect cyberattacks before they happen.

C. Decentralized Identity and Blockchain for Patient Records

- Blockchain can store patient records securely while ensuring only authorized parties can access them.

D. Quantum-Resistant Encryption

- Hospitals and medical device makers must start adopting post-quantum cryptography to future-proof security.

Final Thoughts: The Future of Smart Healthcare Security Is in Our Hands

The future of medical IoT is exciting and terrifying at the same time. On one hand, technology will save more lives than ever. On the other hand, hackers will have more opportunities to exploit healthcare systems than ever before.

So, what's the takeaway? Medical IoT security isn't just about preventing cyberattacks—it's about protecting human lives. Every weak password, outdated system, and unpatched vulnerability could put real patients at risk.

The next decade will be a battle between innovation and exploitation—and it's up to us to make sure security keeps up with progress.

And if your doctor ever tells you that your pacemaker is getting a "software update," maybe double-check who's pushing the update first.

If you've made it to the end of this book, congratulations! You now officially know more about Medical IoT security than most hospital IT departments (which, let's be honest, isn't always saying much). From network attacks to firmware exploitation, ransomware to rogue pacemakers, we've covered how hackers can break into smart healthcare systems—and, more importantly, how to stop them. Hopefully, you're walking away from this with a newfound appreciation for just how fragile yet fixable our connected healthcare world really is.

Medical IoT is both a miracle and a mess. It's saving lives while simultaneously creating some of the most terrifying security risks imaginable. But here's the thing: the more we expose vulnerabilities, the stronger these systems can become. Ethical hackers, security researchers, and cybersecurity professionals (like you, dear reader) are the ones standing between innovation and catastrophe. The future of smart healthcare isn't about avoiding technology—it's about securing it. Because let's be real: no one wants to wake up from surgery only to find their pacemaker has been pwned.

Gratitude and What's Next

First off, a massive thank you for reading this book. Whether you're a seasoned security pro, a curious hacker, or just someone who accidentally bought this book thinking it was a medical drama (hey, it happens), I appreciate you sticking around. The world of IoT security is vast, ever-changing, and occasionally terrifying, but it's people like you—those who care enough to learn—that make it safer for everyone.

If you enjoyed this book (or if it just made you slightly paranoid about your smartwatch), you're in luck. **Hacking Medical IoT** is just one installment in the *IoT Red Teaming: Offensive and Defensive Strategies series*. If you're hungry for more, check out my other books, where we explore everything from **Mastering Hardware Hacking to Drone Hacking to AI-Powered IoT Exploits** (because apparently, AI isn't just coming for our jobs—it's also coming for our smart fridges).

The war between hackers and defenders isn't slowing down, and the best way to stay ahead is to keep learning. Whether you're breaking systems or protecting them, knowledge is your sharpest weapon. So, stay curious, stay ethical (or at least mostly ethical), and always remember: just because something can be hacked, doesn't mean it should be hacked. (Unless, of course, you're ethically hacking it. In that case, hack away.)

Until next time, stay safe, stay secure, and don't trust any device that calls itself "smart."

— *Zephyrion Stravos*